Liza May **Minnelli**, born on March  Angeles, California, U.S., is an act and singer. Best known for her A(performance in Cabaret (1972), she's famous for her energetic stage presence and her powerful mezzo-soprano singing voice, being the daughter of Judy Garland and Vincente Minnelli.

Liza moved to New York City during 1961, looking for theatrical work, where she began her career as a musical theatre actress, nightclub performer and traditional pop music artist. She made her professional stage debut in the Off-Broadway revival of Best Foot Forward in 1963 then won a Tony Award for starring in Flora the Red Menace during 1965. This marked the start of her lifelong collaboration with John Kander and Fred Ebb, who wrote, produced or directed many of Minnelli's future stage acts and TV shows, helping create her stage persona of a stylized survivalist, including her career-defining performances of anthems of survival; 'New York, New York', Cabaret and Maybe This Time. Along with her roles on stage and screen, this persona and her style of performance enhanced Liza's status as an enduring gay icon.

Critically praised for her early non-musical screen performances, particularly in The Sterile Cuckoo (1969), Minnelli rose to international stardom, starring in Cabaret and the Emmy Award-winning TV special Liza with a Z (1972). Most of her following movies, including Lucky Lady (1975), New York, New York (1977), Rent-a-Cop (1988) and Stepping Out (1991), were panned by the critics, having bombed at the box office, Minnelli having had no further big hits except Arthur (1981).

She returned to Broadway a number of times, including in The Act (1977), The Rink (1984) then Liza's at The Palace.... (2008), having also worked in several TV formats, while mainly focusing on music hall and nightclub performances since the late '70s. Minnelli's concert performances at Carnegie Hall in 1979 & 1987 then at Radio City Music Hall during 1991 & 1992 are recognized as among her most successful. From 1988 to 1990, she toured with Frank Sinatra and Sammy Davis Jr. in Frank, Liza & Sammy: The Ultimate Event.

Best known for her renditions of pop standards, Minnelli's early '60s pop singles were produced to attract a young audience then her albums from 1968 to 1977 included much of the contemporary singer-songwriter material. Liza ventured into the contemporary pop scene by collaborating with the Pet Shop Boys on the L.P. Results in 1989. After a break due to serious health problems, Minnelli returned to the concert stage during 2002 with Liza's Back then was an acclaimed guest star in the sitcom Arrested Development from 2003 - 2013. Minnelli has avoided big concert tours during the 2010s, preferring small retrospective performances.

Liza is the daughter of Judy Garland and Vincente Minnelli, her parents having named her after Ira Gershwin's song, Liza (All the Clouds'll Roll Away). She has a half-sister, Lorna, and half-brother, Joey, from Garland's marriage to Sid Luft and another half-sister, Christiane Nina Minnelli, nicknamed Tina Nina, from her father's 2nd marriage. Liza's godparents were Kay Thompson and her husband William Spier.

Her first performing experience on film was at the age of 3, appearing in the final scene of the musical In the Good Old Summertime (1949), the picture starring Judy and Van Johnson. Liza moved to New York City in 1961, attending the High School of Performing Arts, followed by Chadwick School. Minnelli was an apprentice at the Cape Cod Melody Tent in Hyannis, Massachusetts that year, Liza appearing in the chorus of Flower Drum Song then playing the part of Muriel in Take Me Along. She began performing professionally at 17 years old during 1963 in an Off-Broadway revival of the musical Best Foot Forward, for which she received the Theatre World Award.

Garland invited her to perform with her at the London Palladium during the next year, both concerts being recorded then issued as a L.P. Minnelli attended Scarsdale High School for a year, starring in a production of The Diary of Anne Frank, which then went to Israel on tour. She appeared on Broadway at 19, having won her first Tony Award as a leading actress for Flora the Red Menace, the first time that she worked with the musical pair John Kander and Fred Ebb.

Liza began singing in nightclubs as an adolescent, making her professional debut aged 19 at the Shoreham Hotel in Washington, D.C. Minnelli also began appearing in other clubs and on stage in Las Vegas, Los Angeles, Chicago, Miami, and New York City in 1964. Her success as a live performer led to her recording several albums for Capitol Records: Liza! Liza! (1964), It Amazes Me (1965), and There Is a Time (1966).

Minnelli recorded traditional pop standards as well as show tunes from musicals in which she starred during her early years, William Ruhlmann naming her 'Barbra Streisand's little sister'. The Capitol L.Ps Liza! Liza!, It Amazes Me, and There Is A Time were rereleased on the two-CD compilation The Capitol Years in their entirety during 2001. From 1968 to the '70s, she also recorded her L.Ps Liza Minnelli (1968), Come Saturday Morning and New Feelin' (both 1970) for A&M Records then put out The Singer (1973) and Tropical Nights (1977) on Columbia Records.

Minnelli collaborated with the Pet Shop Boys on 'Results' in 1989, an electronic dance-style album, which entered the UK top 10 then charted in the U.S., producing 4 singles: Losing My Mind; Don't Drop Bombs; 'So Sorry, I Said'; and Love Pains. Later that year, Liza performed Losing My Mind live at the Grammys Award ceremony, before receiving a Grammy Legend Award, the first of these being issued during 1990 to Minnelli, Andrew Lloyd Webber, Smokey Robinson, and Willie Nelson. With this award, she became one of only 16 artists, including composer Richard Rodgers, Whoopi Goldberg, Barbra Streisand, and John Gielgud to win an Emmy, Grammy, Tony Award, and Academy Award.

Liza appeared at the tribute concert for her late friend Freddie Mercury during April 1992, performing We Are the Champions with the surviving members of the rock band Queen at Wembley Stadium in London. Minnelli released a studio L.P. titled Gently, a recording of jazz standards, along with contemporary songs including a cover of Does He Love You, which she performed as a duet with Donna Summer, the album receiving a Grammy nomination for Best Traditional Pop Vocal Performance.

Liza was featured on My Chemical Romance's L.P. The Black Parade in 2006, providing backing vocals and singing a solo part with Gerard Way on the track Mama. Minnelli was nominated for Best Traditional Pop Vocal Album during 2009 for her studio recording Liza's at the Palace...!, based on her hit Broadway show. She issued a L.P. on the Decca Records label titled Confessions on September 21st, 2010. The New York Times Magazine of June 25th, 2019 listed Liza Minnelli among hundreds of artists whose material was reportedly destroyed in the Universal fire of 2008.

Minnelli's first appearance on film was as the baby in the very last shot of her mother's movie In the Good Old Summertime (1949). Her first credited film role was as the love-interest in Charlie Bubbles (1967), Albert Finney's only picture as director and star, although 4 years earlier, she provided voiceover work for the animated movie Journey Back to Oz, a sequel to The Wizard of Oz. Liza was the voice of Dorothy, a character played in the earlier film by her mother, in what would've been her first credited movie role had it been released in 1964 as planned—the Filmation production was delayed, eventually being put out in the UK during 1972.

Minnelli appeared in The Sterile Cuckoo (1969), Alan J. Pakula's first picture, as Pookie Adams, a needy, eccentric teenager, her performance being nominated for the Academy Award for Best Actress in a Leading Role. Liza then played another eccentric character in Tell Me That You Love Me, Junie Moon (1970), directed by Otto Preminger. Minnelli appeared in her best-known movie role as Sally Bowles, in the film version of Cabaret (1972).

Liza said that one of the things she did to prepare was to study photographs of actresses Louise Glaum and Louise Brooks, along with dark-haired women of the era in which the picture was set. Minnelli won the Academy Award for Best Actress in a Leading Role for her performance, along with a Golden Globe Award, BAFTA Award, Sant Jordi Award and David di Donatello Award for Best Foreign Actress.

After the success of Cabaret, Bob Fosse and Minnelli teamed up for Liza with a 'Z'. A Concert for Television, a TV special. The program being broadcast twice on TV, not being seen again until a DVD issue in 2006. Minelli appeared in 3 expensive flops in as many years, with Variety suggesting by 1978 that she was # 1 for box office poison. The first was Lucky Lady (1975), then she worked with her father in A Matter of Time (1976), co-starring Ingrid Bergman, followed by New York, New York (1977), which gave Liza her best known signature song. She sometimes performed duets on stage with Frank Sinatra, who recorded a cover version for his Trilogy: Past Present Future album.

Minnelli made fewer movie appearances from then on but her next film, Arthur (1981), in which she starred as Dudley Moore's love interest, was a big hit. She returned to the big screen for Rent-A-Cop and Arthur 2: On the Rocks (both 1988) then Stepping Out (1991), a musical comedy drama. Liza later appeared in The Oh in Ohio during 2006, which only received a limited release in theatres.

Minnelli appeared as a child guest on Art Linkletter's TV show during the '50s, having then sung and danced with Gene Kelly on his first television special in 1959. She was a guest star in one episode of Ben Casey, being a frequent guest on chat shows including many appearances on shows hosted by Jack Paar, Merv Griffin, Mike Douglas, Joe Franklin, Dinah Shore and Johnny Carson.

Liza made several guest appearances on Rowan & Martin's Laugh-In during the '60s, as well as other variety shows including The Ed Sullivan Show, The Hollywood Palace, and The Judy Garland Show. She appeared as Minnie in her first TV dramatic role in the episode Nightingale for Sale on Craig Stevens's short-lived series Mr. Broadway in 1964.

American Public Television aired Liza Minnelli Live from Radio City Music Hall during December 1992, produced by Phil Ramone and Chris Giordano. The show received 6 Emmy nominations, winning the Emmy Award for Outstanding Individual Achievement in Music and Lyrics, awarded to Fred Ebb and John Kander. Minnelli made guest appearances on shows including Arrested Development, Law & Order: Criminal Intent and Drop Dead Diva later in her career.

She appeared on the Ruby Wax, Graham Norton and Jonathan Ross shows in the UK, having taken part in a comedy skit on Charlotte Church's show in October 2006, also being featured on Michael Parkinson's show. American Public Television broadcast Liza's at the Palace in November 2009, taped from September 30th to October 1st, 2009 in Las Vegas, at the MGM Grand's Hollywood Theatre. The executive producers of the taping, Craig Zadan and Neil Meron, had been involved during 2005 with the rerelease of Minnelli's Emmy Award- and Peabody Award-winning Liza with a 'Z' (1972).

Minnelli returned to Broadway in 1997, replacing Julie Andrews in the title role of the musical Victor/Victoria. New York Times critic Ben Brantley wrote in his review, "her every stage appearance is perceived as a victory of show-business stamina over psychic frailty. She asks for love so nakedly and earnestly, it seems downright vicious not to respond".

After a serious case of viral encephalitis during the year 2000, doctors predicted that Liza would spend the rest of her life in a wheelchair, perhaps not being able to speak again. However, by taking vocal and dance lessons daily, mostly with Sam Harris, Ron Lewis, and Angela Bacari, she managed to recover. Minnelli returned to the stage in 2001, when asked by her long-time friend Michael Jackson to perform at Madison Square Garden in New York City, where she sang Never Never Land and the televised You Are Not Alone at the Michael Jackson: 30th Anniversary Special concert, produced by her future husband David Gest. Liza told reporters: "I am stable as a table."

Gest was so impressed with Minnelli's stamina and ability to stun audiences that he produced her in Liza's Back during spring 2002, performing to rave reviews in London and New York City. The tour featured a tribute to her mother: After years of declining fans' pleas for her to sing Garland's signature song Over The Rainbow, she concluded Act 1 with the final refrain of her mother's anthem, receiving an ovation. Amongst performances of her classic hits, other numbers unreleased in the album version included I Believe You by The Carpenters, a rap version of Liza with a Z, Yes, and Mary J. Blige's, Family Affair.

VH1 signed Minnelli and Gest in 2002 to appear in a reality show titled Liza and David. The pilot episode was filmed following the couple around as they prepared for a party at their home, with a guest list including Ray Charles, Luther Vandross, Isaac Mizrahi, Anastacia, and others. However, the show was cancelled shortly after the pilot episode was completed due to a dispute between VH1 with Gest and Minnelli, never being broadcast, although recordings of the pilot episode still exist.

Liza appeared from 2003 - 2005, as a recurring character on the Emmy Award-winning TV sitcom Arrested Development as Lucille Austero, also known as Lucille 2, the lover of both the sexually and socially awkward Buster Bluth and Buster's brother

Gob. Minnelli later appeared in the role for the show's 4th season during 2013.

Liza made a guest appearance during September 2006, on the long-running drama Law & Order: Criminal Intent in 'Masquerade', a Halloween-themed episode, which was broadcast on October 31st, 2006. Minnelli also completed guest vocals on My Chemical Romance's concept L.P. The Black Parade that year, portraying 'Mother War', a dark conception of the main character's mother in the song 'Mama'.

She returned to Broadway in a new solo concert at the Palace Theatre titled Liza's at The Palace...!, which ran from December 3rd, 2008 to January 4th, 2009, performing a series of numbers created by Kay Thompson in her 2nd act. The reviews observed that while Minnelli's voice was ragged at times, with her movements no longer being elastic, the old magic was still very much present. The show was then staged at the MGM Grand in Las Vegas from September 30th to October 1st, 2009, being filmed for broadcast on public TV, with a February 2010 DVD and Blu-ray issue.

Liza made a rare surprise appearance on live TV on January 10th, 2009, on Saturday Night Live, playing the best friend of Penelope (Kristen Wiig). Minnelli was then on The View on January 26th, singing 'I Would Never Leave You', written by Johnny Rodgers, Billy Stritch, and Brian Lane Green, from her CD, Liza's at The Palace...!, also being interviewed by the cast of The View.

Minnelli was a character in the Australian musical The Boy from Oz, a biography of her first husband, starring Hugh Jackman, having been portrayed by Stephanie J. Block in the show's Broadway production. Liza toured Australia in October 2009, appearing on Australian Idol as a mentor and guest judge then appeared in a Snickers advert along with Aretha Franklin and Betty White during February 2010.

She made a cameo appearance in that May's release of Sex and the City 2, in which she covered Beyoncé's hit Single Ladies (Put a Ring on It) and Cole Porter's Ev'ry Time We Say Goodbye. Minnelli starred in The Apprentice in December 2010, having also issued an 'unplugged' album of American standards that year with long time collaborator Billy Stritch, showing a sultrier, softer, more interpretive side to her artistry. The songs were said to have been recorded several years previously, later released as the L.P. Confessions.

Liza headlined at Hampton Court Palace Festival on June 14th, 2012 then was a guest artist on Cher's Dressed to Kill Tour in Brooklyn on May 9th, 2014, performing Girls Just Want to Have Fun with Cyndi Lauper and Rosie O'Donnell. Minnelli performed at the IP Casino Resort & Spa on July 24th, 2015, celebrating the 50th anniversary of the closing of Flora the Red Menace.

Liza has long suffered from alcoholism, having been addicted to prescription drugs, beginning with a Valium prescription following her mother's death. Her use of recreational drugs during the '70s was observed by Andy Warhol, who in a diary entry in 1978 recalled Minnelli arriving at Halston's house then imploring the host to "Give me every drug you've got." Liza made frequent appearances at New York City nightclubs with Warhol and Bianca Jagger during the late '70s. Minnelli left her musical The Rink during 1984 to enter the Betty Ford Clinic.

The family moved the remains of Liza's mother, Judy Garland, from Ferncliff Cemetery in Greenburgh, Westchester County, New York to Hollywood Forever Cemetery in Los Angeles, California in 2017. Minneli has stated that she's an Episcopalian.

Liza's friendships have included the singer Adam Ant, whom she advised on what to wear when he was presented to Queen Elizabeth II after the Royal Variety Performance of 1981, at which his band Adam and the Ants performed. Ant in turn namechecked Minnelli in the track Crackpot History and the Right To Lie on his solo album Friend or Foe.

Liza has got wed and divorced 4 times, her first marriage having been to entertainer Peter Allen on March 3rd, 1967. Australian-born Allen was Judy Garland's protégé in the mid-'60s. The couple divorced on July 24th, 1974, Minnelli having told The Advocate editor-in-chief Judy Wieder during September 1996 "I married Peter, and he didn't tell me he was gay. Everyone knew but me, and I found out ... well, let me put it this way: I'll never surprise anybody coming home as long as I live. I call first!".

Liza wed Jack Haley Jr., a producer and director, on September 15th, 1974, whose father, Jack Haley, was Garland's co-star in The Wizard of Oz, the pair divorcing in April 1979. Minnelli was married to Mark Gero, a sculptor and stage manager, from December 4th that year until their divorce during January 1992. Liza wed David Gest, a concert promoter, on March 16th, 2002, the couple separating in July 2003 then divorcing during April 2007.

Gest brought a lawsuit in 2003, alleging that Minnelli beat him in alcohol-induced rages during their marriage. Liza also had relationships with Rock Brynner, son of Yul Brynner, Desi Arnaz, Jr., Peter Sellers, and Martin Scorsese. Minnelli has no children; one pregnancy having left her with a hiatal hernia due to the medical steps taken to try to save the baby.

Throughout her lifetime, Liza has supported charities and causes, having served on the board of directors of The Institutes for The Achievement of Human Potential (IAHP) for 20 years, a nonprofit educational organization that introduces parents to the field of child brain development. In an interview with Randy Rice at Broadwayworld.com during 2006, Minnelli said that she told Elizabeth Taylor about HIV/AIDS, while talking about their mutual friend Rock Hudson.

She's also dedicated a lot of time to amfAR, The Foundation for AIDS Research, which was co-founded by Taylor. Liza said in an interview with Palm Springs Life in 2007: "AmfAR is important to me because I've lost so many friends that I knew [to AIDS]". She recorded the Kander & Ebb tune The Day After That during 1994, donating the proceeds to AIDS research. That same year, Minnelli performed the song in front of thousands in Central Park, at the 25th anniversary of the Stonewall riots.

Discography

Studio albums

Liza! Liza! (1964)

It Amazes Me (1965)

There Is a Time (1966)

Liza Minnelli (1968)

Come Saturday Morning (1969)

New Feelin' (1970)

The Singer (1973)

Tropical Nights (1977)

Results (1989)

Gently (1996)

Confessions (2010)

Filmography

Acting

Year	Title	Role	Notes
1949	In the Good Old Summertime	Veronica and Andrew's Daughter	uncredited role
1964	Mr. Broadway	Minnie	Episode: Nightingale for Sale
1967	Charlie Bubbles	Eliza	
1968	That's Life	secretary	Episode: Twas the Night Before Christmas

Year	Title	Role	Notes
1969	The Sterile Cuckoo	Mary Ann 'Pookie' Adams	nominated – Academy Award for Best Actress
1970	Tell Me That You Love Me, Junie Moon	Junie Moon	
1972	Cabaret	Sally Bowles	Academy Award for Best Actress
1972	Journey Back to Oz	Dorothy Gale (voice)	Recorded in 1962, released in the U.S. in 1974
1975	Lucky Lady	Claire	
1976	A Matter of Time	Nina	
1977	New York, New York	Francine Evans	
1981	Arthur	Linda Marolla	
1984	Faerie Tale Theatre	Princess Alecia	Episode: "The Princess and the Pea"
1985	A Time to Live	Mary-Lou Weisman	TV movie
1988	Rent-a-Cop	Della Roberts	
	Arthur 2: On the Rocks	Linda Marolla Bach	
1991	Stepping Out	Mavis Turner	
1994	Parallel Lives	Stevie Merrill	TV movie
1995	The West Side Waltz	Cara Varnum	TV movie
2003–05			
2013	Arrested Development	Lucille Austero	21 episodes

2006   The Oh in Ohio   Alyssa Donahue

2006   Law & Order: Criminal Intent   Beth Harner Episode: Masquerade

2009   Drop Dead Diva Lily Wells   Episode: "Make Me a Match"

As herself

Year   Title   Notes

1963   The Judy Garland Show   Episode: The Judy Garland Christmas Special

1964   Judy and Liza at the Palladium   TV special with Judy Garland

1965   The Dangerous Christmas of Red Riding Hood   TV special

1970   Liza   TV special

1972   Liza with a "Z": A Concert for Television   Special

1974   Love from A to Z   TV special with Charles Aznavour

1974   That's Entertainment!   host

1976   Silent Movie   cameo appearance

1979   The Muppet Show   Episode: Liza Minnelli

1980   Goldie and Liza Together   TV special with Goldie Hawn

1980   An Evening with Liza Minnelli   TV special

1983   The King of Comedy   credit only

1984   The Muppets Take Manhattan   cameo appearance

1985   That's Dancing! host

1986   Liza in London   TV special

1987   Minnelli on Minnelli: Liza Remembers Vincente   documentary

1988   Sam Found Out: A Triple Play   TV special

1989   Frank, Liza & Sammy: The Ultimate Event   TV special with Frank Sinatra and Sammy Davis Jr.

1992   The Freddie Mercury Tribute Concert for AIDS Awareness   TV special

1992   Liza Live from Radio City Music Hall   TV special

1993   Liza and Friends: A Tribute to Sammy Davis Jr.   special (with Charles Aznavour, Tom Jones, Jerry Lewis & Cliff Richard)

1999   Jackie's Back   TV film (cameo appearance)

2010   Sex and the City 2   cameo appearance

2013   Smash   Episode: The Surprise Party

Stage productions

Year   Title   Role   Notes

1961   Wish You Were Here   Ballet solo   Cape Cod Melody Tent, Hyannis, Massachusetts

1961   Take Me Along   Muriel   Cape Cod Melody Tent, Hyannis, Massachusetts

1961   Flower Drum Song   chorus   Cape Cod Melody Tent, Hyannis, Massachusetts

1961–1962   The Diary of Anne Frank   Anne Frank   Scarsdale High School, Scarsdale, New York and Israel Tour

1963   Best Foot Forward   Ethel Hofflinger   Off-Broadway (Stage 73, New York City)

1964   Carnival!   Lili   Paper Mill Playhouse, Millburn, New Jersey

1964   Time Out For Ginger   Ginger   Bucks County Playhouse, New Hope, Pennsylvania

1964   The Fantasticks   Luisa   US National Tour

1965   Flora the Red Menace   Flora   Broadway (Alvin Theatre, New York City)

1966   The Pajama Game   Babe Williams   US National Tour

1974   Liza   herself (one-woman show)   Broadway (Winter Garden Theatre, New York City)

1975   Chicago   Roxie Hart   Broadway (46th Street Theatre, New York City)

Note: replacement for Gwen Verdon

Year	Production	Role	Venue
1977–1978	The Act	Michelle Craig	Broadway (Majestic Theatre, New York City)
1978	Are You Now or Have You Ever Been?	Letter Reader (cameo)	Off-Broadway (Promenade Theatre, New York City)
1978–1979	The Owl and the Pussycat	The Storyteller	Metropolitan Opera House (Lincoln Center), New York City
1984	The Rink	Angel	Broadway (Martin Beck Theatre, New York City)
1994	Love Letters	Melissa Gardner	Coconut Grove Playhouse, Miami, Florida
1997	Victor/Victoria	Victoria Grant	Broadway (Marquis Theatre, New York City)

Note: vacation replacement for Julie Andrews

Year	Production	Role	Venue
1999–2000	Minnelli on Minnelli: Live at the Palace	herself (one-woman show)	Broadway (Palace Theatre, New York City)
2008–2009	Liza's at The Palace....	herself (one-woman show)	Broadway (Palace Theatre, New York City)
2013	Liza's and Alan	herself	Broadway (Town Hall, New York City)

Further reading

Leigh, Wendy (1993), Liza: Born a Star. E.P. Dutton

Mair, George (1996), Under the Rainbow: The Real Liza Minnelli. Carol Publishing

Schechter, Scott (2004), The Liza Minnelli Scrapbook. Kensington Books/Citadel Press

Spada, James (1983), Judy and Liza. Doubleday

Wimmer, Martin (2018), Clockwork Liza. Star und Künstlerin: Das Lebenswerk der Liza Minnelli. BoD-Books on Demand

Liza Minnelli had largely withdrawn from public view over the past few years, leading to tabloid speculation about her declining health, headlines that had dogged her for much of her life and career. However, the 72-year-old showgal was stepping back into the spotlight for an intimate evening of songs and conversation with longtime confidante and musical collaborator Michael Feinstein, at Segerstrom Center for the Arts in Orange County, California. The event had been scheduled take place in Las Vegas on March 30th, but 4 days before the performance an email had been sent out informing ticket holders that the show was being canceled because 'Ms. Minnelli is suffering from an extreme viral infection', fueling more speculation.

Feinstein later stated that Liza was 'Feeling fine. She's sober. She's happy. She's partying with Darren Criss and most importantly — she's doing whatever she damn well pleases'.

What had happened?

'The concert in Vegas was canceled because Liza had to go into the hospital for a couple of days. She felt so bad about it, because she's very mindful of her reputation. Especially these days where she doesn't appear very often. She wanted so much to be there, but things happen'.

How's Minnelli's health?

'She's feeling very good now and we both are very excited about this show, because it will be the first time that she's done anything where she's appeared in a casual setting, singing songs extemporaneously and taking questions from the audience'.

What was Liza going to sing?

'What she said the other day is that she wants to do what she calls her 'chair songs'. She always does a segment in her show where she sits in this director's chair and does these acting pieces, like material by Charles Aznavour, which are acting pieces that are lyrically driven, like You've Let Yourself Go, What Makes a Man a Man. In addition to some of her standards or chestnuts'.

Like Cabaret?

'Yes, of course. She won't disappoint her audience'.

It was Minnelli's first live performance for a long while. Had it become too exhausting?

"It's not that it's too exhausting. It's that she's done it for 60 years and she's at a point now where she's actually taking time to relax and enjoy her life. She moved to Los Angeles a couple of years ago and she's decided that she wants to have some fun. She's always obediently followed the directive of her managers and agents and she's tired of it. She's been sober for many years and she's been taking stock in her life. Her priorities are different. She says, 'I wake up every morning and I think, 'What do I have to do today? Nothing'".

Did Liza enjoy living in Los Angeles?

"For years she told me that she'd never move back but her life has changed to a point where all the ghosts that used to bother her about being here have dissipated. From the moment that I met her she seemed like the quintessential New Yorker in the way she lived but she loves the gentler lifestyle in L.A. and a lot of her friends are here".

Who were they nowadays?

"She's close to Michelle Lee and she's close to George Hamilton. Marisa Berenson's daughter had a baby, so Marisa — who did Cabaret with Liza — comes to California from Paris quite often. They'll see each other whenever she's here. Michael York, also from Cabaret, she loves him. Recently we had a little party and I introduced Liza to Darren Criss and his fiancee Mia Swier, because Darren is a big Liza fan. They kind of fell in love with each other, so I think Darren will become part of the parties that we have where we have music and just kind of hang out. It's a lot of fun".

She made a rare statement on Facebook, distancing herself from the new movie Judy, starring Renee Zellweger as her legendary mother Judy Garland. Had Minnelli spoken about that at all?

"She has talked about it. The important thing to note is that it was a specific response to an article Radar Online posted. For years they've posted stories that she's dying but they published another story stating that she spent several hours on the phone with Renee Zellweger, is coaching her on how to play her mother, that they fell in love with each other and how happy she is with the movie.

Which is total fiction and even though Liza's policy has been to ignore stuff like that, it really irritated her that Radar and other publications have gotten so ballsy about quoting things that she never said. TMZ quoted something about Lady Gaga that she never said. She loves Lady Gaga, but it just happened that she never said what they quoted about A Star Is Born. She wanted to respond, because otherwise that fictitious Radar article would've been repeated and published all over the globe. So that's why she made that statement, because she's never met Renee Zellweger".

It didn't sound like Minnelli wanted the movie to exist at all.

"She's not happy about it, because the producer said it was going to be in the same vein as this play that was on Broadway a few years ago that was horrifying, because it was this fictitious imagining of Judy Garland's last days on earth, with all of this bullsh*t dialogue that was created. There were tragic aspects to her mother's life, no question but her mother also lived very joyously. People never emphasize those things. So it's a no-win as the daughter of Judy Garland to see something like that happen. As she put it, 'The greatest tribute to my mother is to watch her own movies, not a film about her. No one can sing like Mama!'"

How about an authorized Broadway musical based on Liza's life? There'd already been one about her ex-husband Peter Allen — 'The Boy From Oz', starring Hugh Jackman — followed by others about Cher and Donna Summer over the past year.

"She'd never authorize that. She said to me, 'Michael, you can say anything you want about me after I'm dead'. She tells me lots of stories about her that are confidential. People are constantly portraying her in shows around the world and it's very painful for her. She doesn't want to see somebody do her. She says, 'Honey, not when I'm alive and can still do it'".

When the announcement came, at c. 3:15 pm on Sunday, you could feel the audience tensing at the Marquis Theater. "We're experiencing a technical difficulty', said the voice, unreassuringly smooth, on the loudspeaker. It was a statement that always chilled the blood of theatregoers, but especially those who'd come from out of town expressly to see a big star. The woman behind hissed anxiously, 'Do you think they mean Liza?'

Minutes later came a 2nd announcement: 'Ladies and gentlemen, at this performance, the role of Victoria Grant, usually played by Julie Andrews, will be played by Liza Minnelli'. The following roar from the crowd was of the sort one normally heard in baseball stadiums. Ms. Minnelli wasn't even onstage yet, but she had already hit a home run.

Liza, who was indeed filling in for Ms. Andrews in the title role of the musical 'Victor/Victoria' through Feb. 2nd, had an intense relationship with her fans that was without parallel in the theatre. The daughter of Judy Garland, the great, famously troubled singer and actress, she'd had her own, intensely publicized personal and medical problems - stays in rehab centres, hip replacement surgery - with her every stage appearance being perceived as a victory of show-business stamina over psychic frailty.

Like Peter Pan's fairy pal, Tinkerbell, Minnelli seemed to need applause to be brought fully into existence. Sally Field, accepting her 2nd Oscar, memorably gasped: "I can't deny the fact that you like me -- right now, you like me!' but the sentiments behind those words underlay Liza's every gesture as a performer. She asked for love so nakedly and earnestly, it seemed downright vicious not to respond.

As it turned out, this sensibility served 'Victor/Victoria' quite well, making it a different experience from when Ms. Andrews was presiding, who returned to the show the following month. Minnelli didn't raise the standard of the show about a woman who impersonated a female impersonator. It remained a clumsy leer of a musical but she definitely raised its emotional temperature.

As directed by Blake Edwards, who adapted the show's book from his movie of the same title, 'Victor/Victoria' had always been little more than a pedestal for its star. Ever elegant and efficient, Julie, who was married to Blake, reigned from that pedestal with radiant and unfailing poise. The comfort of watching her came from knowing that no matter how vulgar the proceedings around her, she'd never be tarnished by them. Even performing the show's parts of low comedy, she seemed somehow above them and you never worried that her Victoria

Grant would be able to pull off the fraud on which the show was built.

Liza, in contrast, who'd been in the production for under a week, her first appearance in a Broadway musical for over a decade, appeared visibly nervous when she arrived onstage, trembling and gasping in a manner that bordered on hyperventilation but then her character, a small-time singer out of a job, was supposed to be nervous at that point. As the clapping that greeted her entrance mounted, Minnelli seemed to relax into it, as though it were a warm bath. Suddenly, 'Victor/Victoria' became a rooting show, with the audience's concerns for the star and her character blurring into one empathic response.

So what if her dancing seemed a tad uncertain? Who cared if Liza's voice wandered strangely in her harmonies with her co-stars Tony Roberts and Michael Nouri? So what if she looked like a cute toy penguin when she wore a tuxedo? Lacking Andrews's cool androgyny, Minnelli was actually funnier when pretending to be a man. She brought a welcome earthiness to her comic timing and a touching haplessness to Victoria's confusion.

As always, Liza's voice, of a limited range, tended to circle notes before finally landing on them but it remained a big, heartfelt voice, best showcased in the new song, 'Who Can I Tell?,' composed by Frank Wildhorn, that did more than justice to the bland melodies of Henry Mancini and the appallingly strained lyrics of Leslie Briscusse. When she stood onstage, alone in the spotlight, her hair slicked back, her hands clenched and her voice at full throttle, Minnelli inevitably evoked her mother in her fabled late concert appearances.

At the show's beginning, Liza's character admonished, "There are still professions in which practice does indeed make perfect'. Doubtless her performance, raw in its early days, would acquire polish as she continued in her run, but it was the rawness as much as the polish that brought her admirers to the Marquis.

Was this really Liza Minnelli? She looked like no picture of Minnelli ever seen - not Liza in her gorgeous young Cabaret bloom, nor the bloated Minnelli of recent years, nor anything in between. She looked slim and well-preserved for the age of 62, but the great dark eyes that used to be her trademark had vanished into the surrounding orange mask. She could've been almost any woman who'd had extensive plastic surgery but it would've been rude to ask to see her passport. It didn't help that there was an audience in the room - her publicist, a woman Liza introduced as a friend, along with a TV crew waiting to film her for The South Bank Show.

The other problem was that although Minnelli had been famous for ever - born into Hollywood royalty and a star in her own right from her teens - her inquisitor had almost entirely missed her career, having seen her in Cabaret but that was about it. Liza had always seemed to belong to an older generation; having been singing with Frank Sinatra and Sammy Davis Jnr while her age group were listening to the Beatles and even by her 20s, she was already a 'gay icon', just like her mother. When asked why she thought that was, Minnelli said it was because 'gays have good taste!', but maybe it had more to do with having shared her mother's mistake of marrying gay men - her first husband, Peter Allen, was supposed to have been the lover of Judy Garland's 4th husband, Mark Herron.

However, Liza had a huge, devoted fan base, which had already snapped up most of the tickets for her forthcoming UK tour, beginning at the London Coliseum on 25th May. It was billed as her first British tour for 25 years, although she'd toured there in 1986, having been back for concerts in London many times. The first half of the show was, Minnelli said, "Just songs that I like and a couple that people ask me to sing, because I'm not a record act. The only hit record I ever had was with the wonderful Pet Shop Boys here ['Losing My Mind', 1988]. I never had one in America, but it's all right, I sell out anyway!"

The 2nd half of the show was a departure, a 45-minute piece titled 'The Godmother and the Goddaughter' about Liza's relationship with her real-life godmother Kay Thompson, who was probably known lately, if at all, as the author of Eloise at the Plaza but, Minnelli said, "She's an underground hero in showbusiness. She was the first one ever to understand a certain kind of harmony in a song". Kay did all MGM's vocal arrangements in their golden years and had a hugely influential radio show.

Thompson later had a nightclub act which Liza remembered seeing when she was aged 3: "It was amazing. I was sitting on my mum's lap, across from my father to see Kay Thompson at Ciro's and I always remember this energy force, this woman flying around the room and singing these harmonies so everyone went, 'Wow!' So I thought, 'That's what I want to do'. People who don't even know about Kay, I want to show them what I saw - that incredible drive, that sense of humour, that wit. She was so funny".

Kay was originally a friend of Judy Garland's but took over as a sort of surrogate mother to Minnelli after Garland's death during 1967 and Thompson was staying at Liza's house when she'd died 10 years earlier. So it was Minnelli's musical tribute to her godmother, which she planned to record as a TV special when the tour was finished. Liza said she'd been rehearsing and 'building' the show for 9 months.

"It's like being an athlete; you get into a certain shape, where you really have the right wind, because it's all to do with breath, as singing and dancing at the same time isn't easy! The whole 2nd half is all dance routines". Hadn't Minnelli had a hip replacement? "Two, and a wired-up knee. I've got 2 crushed discs too. Never stop moving or you'll stop moving. I go to dance class every morning and it's just good to stay strong; I like being healthy".

There'd been newspaper reports that Liza had collapsed during a concert in Sweden just before Christmas, having had to cancel the rest of her Scandinavian tour, so what happened? "Look!" she opened her mouth, baring her teeth. They looked fine. "I've got 4 of them missing. I had serious, serious - they took out part of my jaw, they took out all of these teeth! and because I'm a dancer, I don't complain, you just don't complain, so I was thinking, 'Ow, this really hurts!' then I went to the doctor and said, 'Please give me something, this hurts me so much', but it had a bridge over, so you couldn't see anything then he said, 'Yer yer yer" [Swedish accent] and I don't know what the hell he gave me, but I waltzed around that stage! It was horrendous". Minnelli talked in a kind of breathless rush that often seemed to miss out key connections.

She'd had more than her fair share of health problems; apart from the hip replacements, the wired-up knee, the crushed vertebrae and an operation for polyps on her vocal cords in

1997, which left her unable to sing for 18 months, she'd been in and out of rehab for years, attending AA and generally 'battling with her demons'. Liza said of her alcoholism: "My whole life, this disease has been rampant. I inherited it, and it's been horrendous, but I've always asked for help". She'd also had problems with prescription drugs, which she said had started when a doctor put her on Valium after her mother's death. Andy Warhol's diary recorded Minnelli turning up at fashion designer Halston's house in 1978, imploring: "Give me every drug you've got!" then him obligingly handing over coke, marijuana, Valium and 4 Quaaludes.

However, Liza's most serious health setback had come in the year 2000, when she contracted encephalitis from a mosquito bite, being told that she'd spend the rest of her life in a wheelchair: "I had to learn to walk again, had to learn to talk again. People don't usually recover like I recovered but I wouldn't give up. I just couldn't - I don't know how you'd do anything else. I was lying there, scared, and my father always told me, 'The way you do something is you think about it'. So on the wall, when they turned my head there was a pattern of leaves and I started to count them and I was going 'Ah ah ah' until I could say them then I did the same thing with walking. I really worked to get back. Most people don't come through it".

One wondered at times if the encephalitis had left Minnelli with amnesia, as the way she described her childhood bore no relation to the account given in biographies of her and her mother. Despite growing up in the heart of Hollywood, she said: "We were brought up to be as normal as possible. It was so much more normal than anybody else I'd ever met. It was a very scheduled life - breakfast at 7am, go to school, it was very organised, very reassuring and not wacky at all. I'm sorry to disappoint but it wasn't wacky!"

Hadn't Liza been exposed to the ups and down of showbiz? "I don't even know what you mean by exposed. I was right there in the heart of it, but exposed? No. That's where I grew up. If my parents were coalminers, I'd have grown up in a mining town and I had no interest in filming. I sometimes went to the studios with my dad but it was slow-going; it was boring to watch. I always ended up in the rehearsal hall watching the dancing. That's what I liked to do".

Her parents split up when Minnelli was aged 5, but she said that was fine - "They married again so many times I've millions of parents". By the time she was 13 years old, she had a stepfather, a stepmother, a stepbrother, a half-sister from her father and another half-sister & half-brother from her mother, many of whom she was expected to look after. Liza was usually the one who had to cope with her mother's addictions, severe depressions and frequent suicide attempts. She stated that the suicide attempts were " Just silly things to attract attention", but still they must've been frightening for a child to witness.

Minnelli also went to 14 different schools, which couldn't have helped, so her parents didn't object when, aged 16, she announced that she was moving to New York to live alone while trying to make a stage career. Her parents said OK - but they wouldn't support her, Frank Sinatra sending her $500 but she sent it back. Liza really did support herself, which meant sometimes doing a runner from hotels without paying, a habit she'd picked up from her mother, and once or twice sleeping on park benches but by the time she was 19 years old, she'd won a

Tony award for her first musical, Flora the Red Menace then aged 26 won an Oscar for Cabaret.

Minnelli once said, possibly quoting her mother, that "Reality is something you have to rise above", which seemed to be what she'd done with her childhood - banished the bad bits and remembered the good. Anyway, she wasn't interested in the past, having once said that she would never have analysis, because "there are doors I don't want opened". Liza prided herself on the fact that, whereas her mother was always making cries for help, she'd always been self-reliant. As she often emphasized, she was her father's daughter too - she was far happier talking about Vincente Minnelli than about Judy Garland. She liked to say that her mother gave her her drive, her father her dreams.

Both parents seemed to have given her a very cavalier attitude to marriage - Liza often having had very public affairs while still married to someone else. Andy Warhol observed in his diary during 1978: 'Her life's very complicated now. Like she was walking down the street with Jack Haley, her husband, and they'd run into Martin Scorsese, who she's now having an affair with, and Marty attacked her for also having an affair with [Mikhail] Baryshnikov... this is going on with her husband standing there!' Jack Haley was Minnelli's husband number two and straight, but they were friends rather than lovers.

Husband number three, Mark Gero, a sculptor, was the one she hoped to have children with, but after three bad miscarriages Liza gave up. Then there was her gripping 4th wedding to David Gest in 2002, known as the Night of a 1,000 Facelifts, with Liz Taylor, Mia Farrow and Michael Jackson as bridesmaids. Their marriage lasted for just over a year, but the divorce case much longer, Gest having accused her of beating him up.

Perhaps, more pertinently, he stated that she was 'unable to be effectively merchandised' because she was 'alcoholic and overweight'. Minnelli in turn accused him of drugging her, of being 'a manipulative neat freak' and putting her dog down. There was also a suit from a bodyguard who alleged that she harassed him with sexual demands but she said she'd never marry again: "I'm adamant about it. There's no reason on this earth". So why had she married as often as she did? "Because I kept trying to get it right and I never did, so I gave up!" Why had she ever thought David was right?

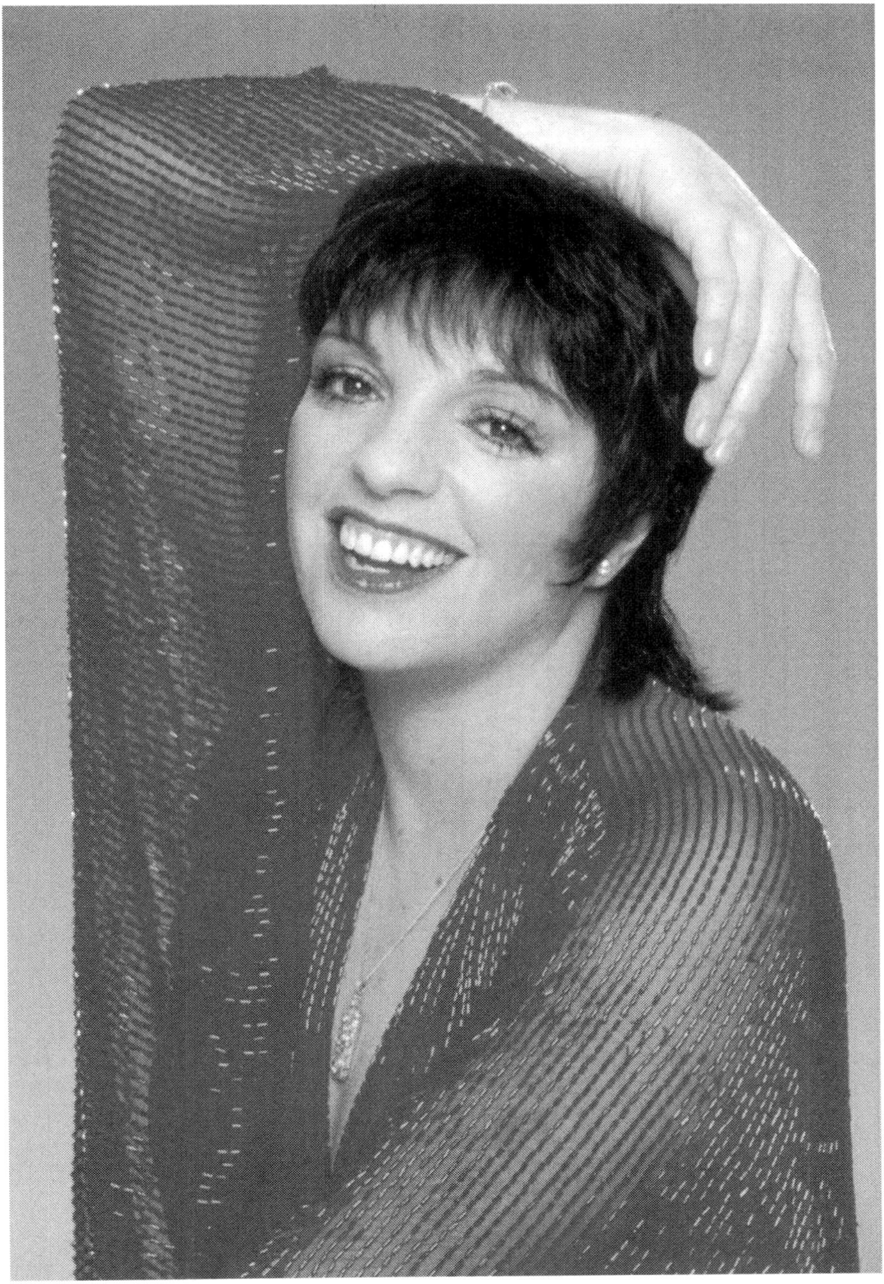

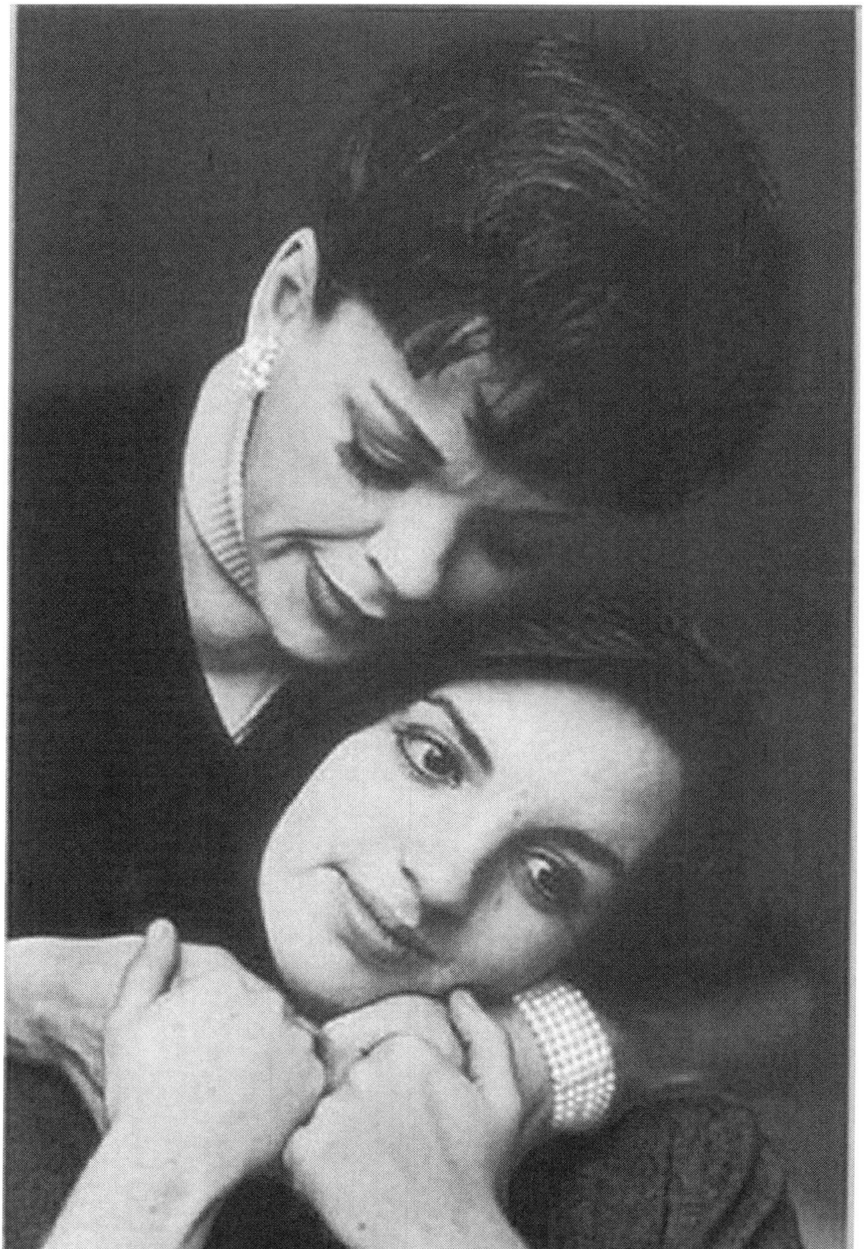

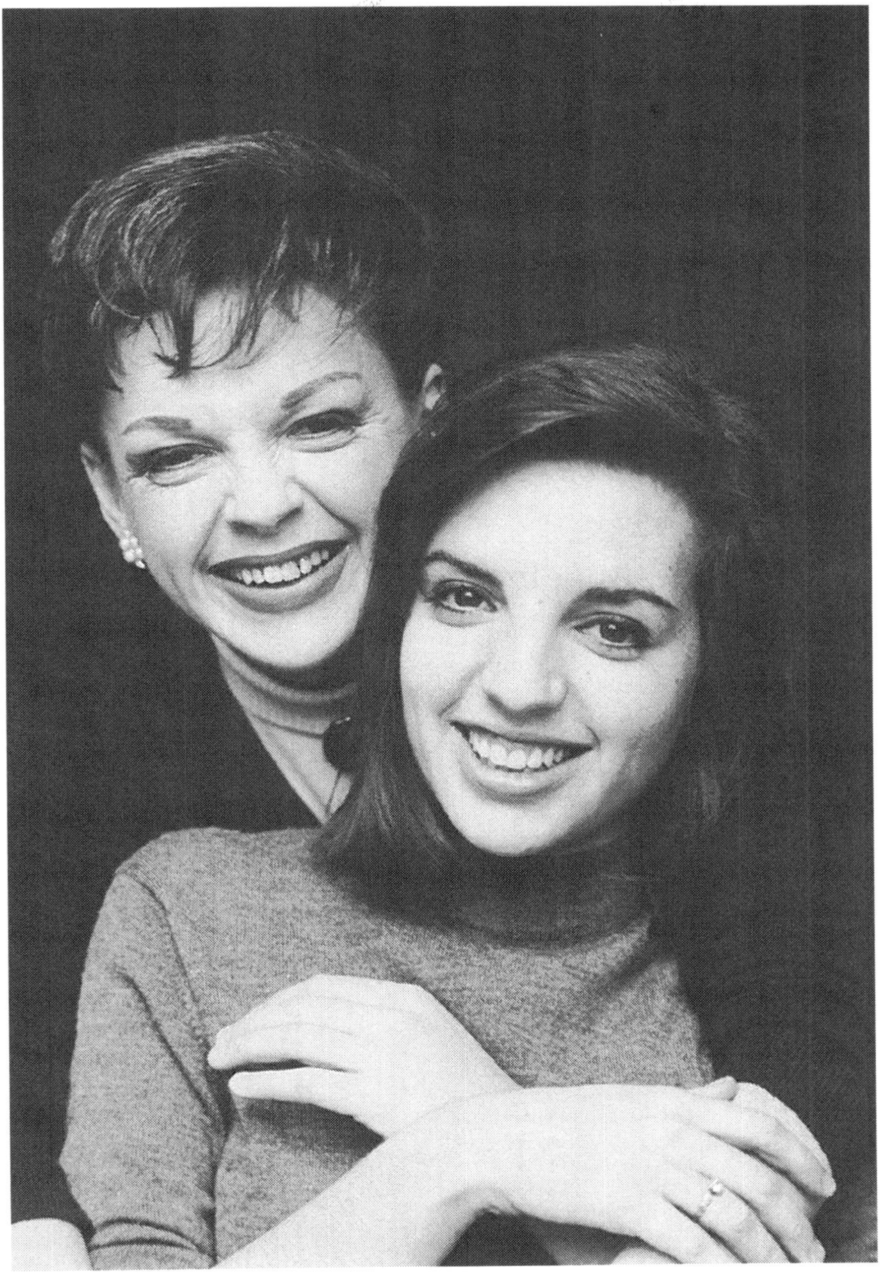

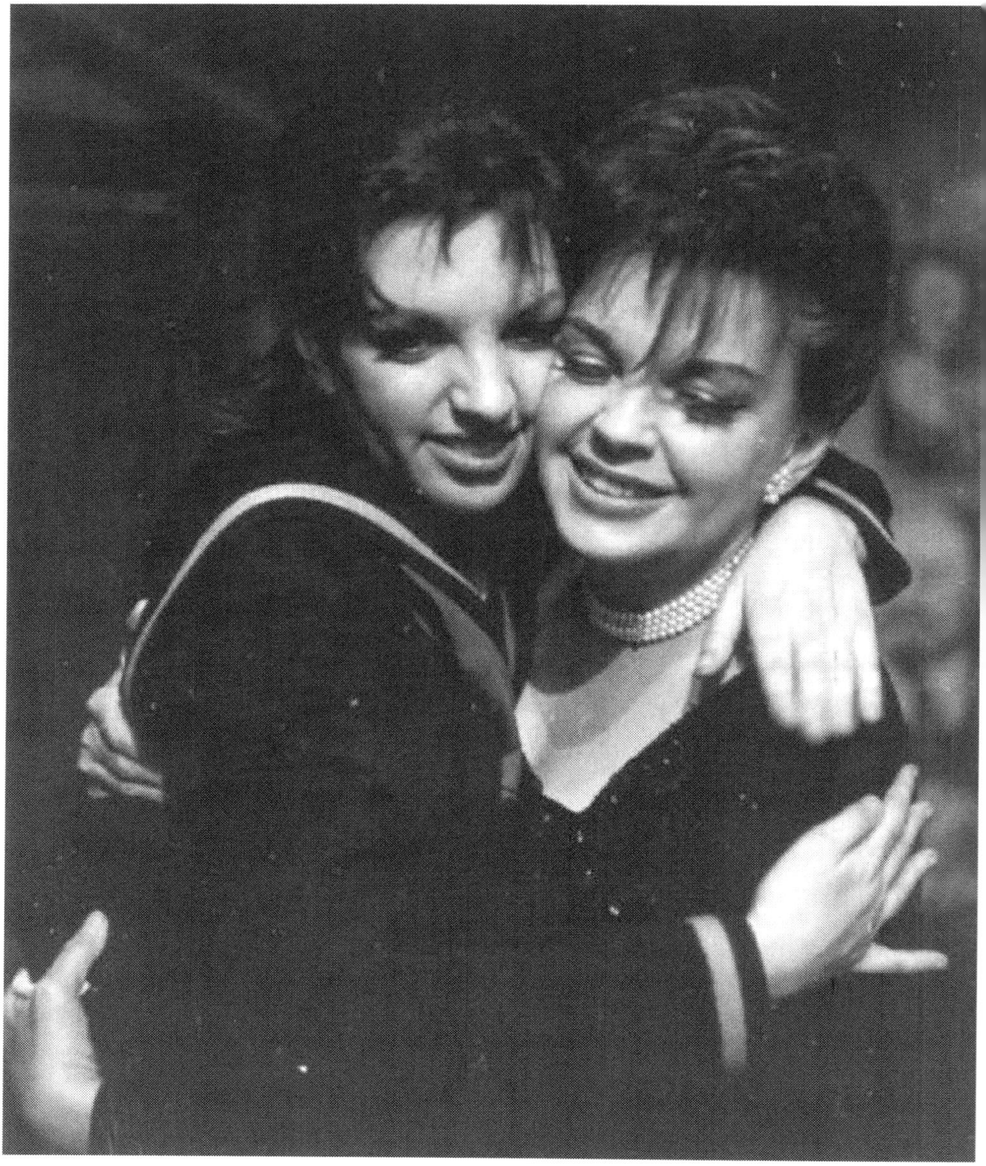

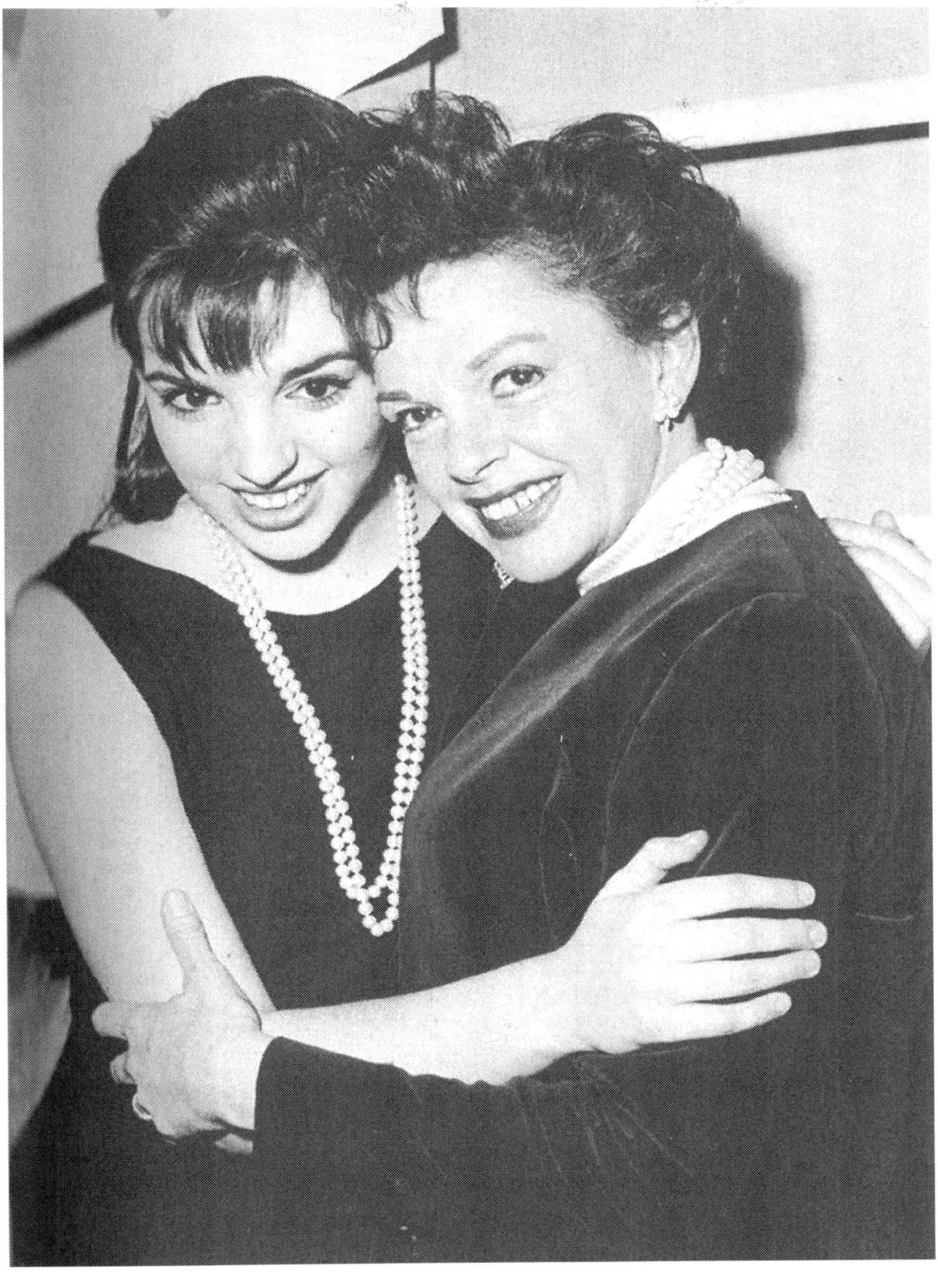

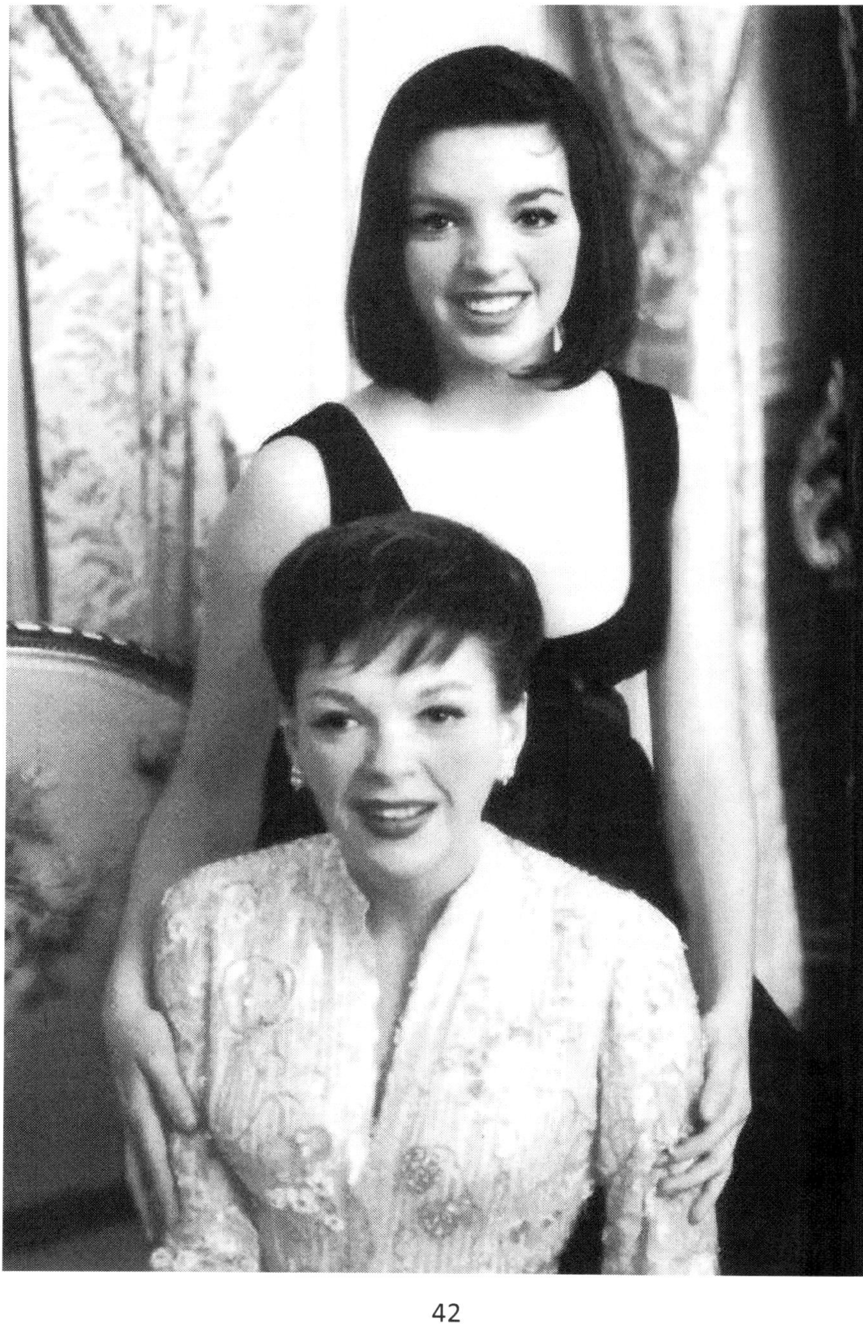

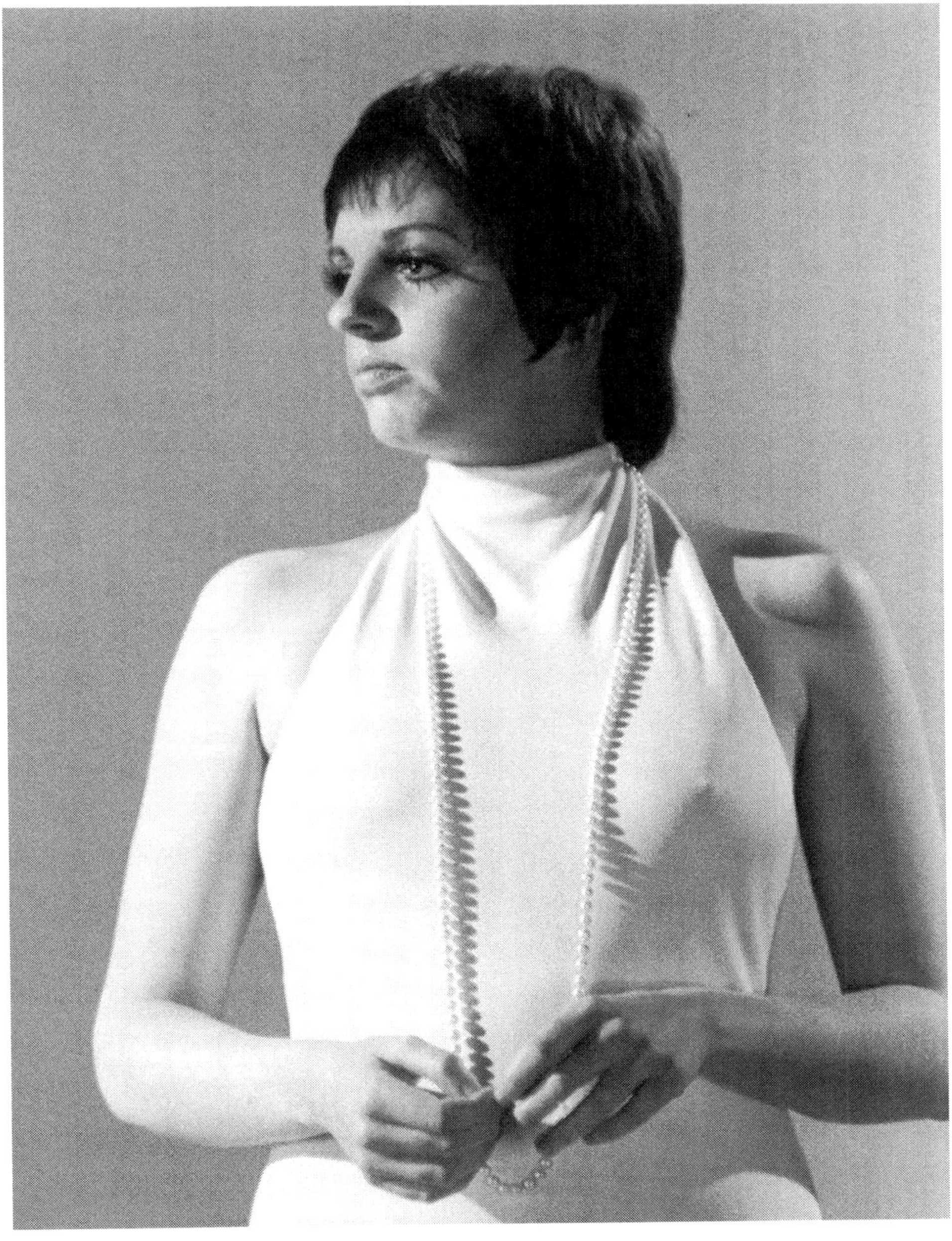

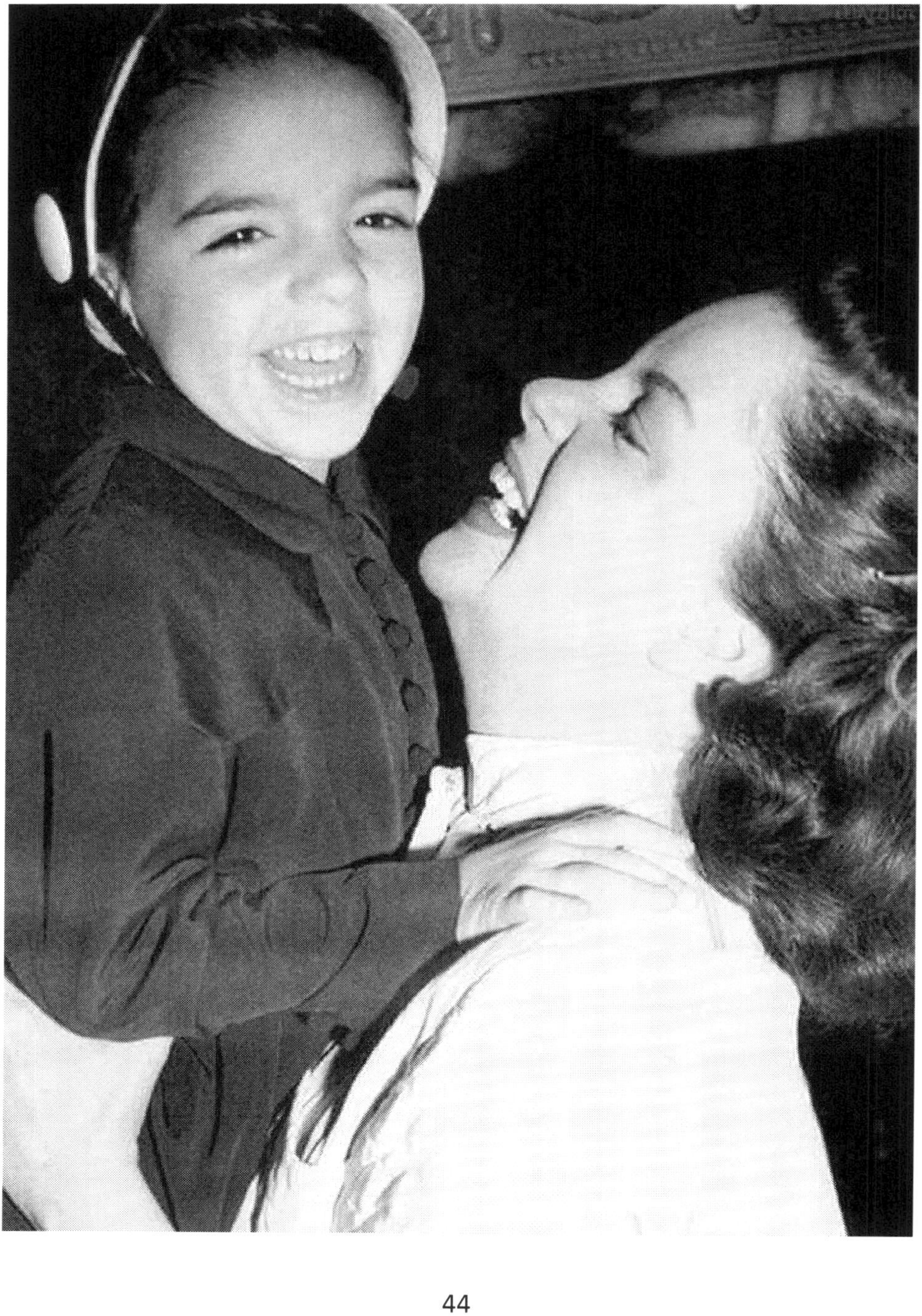

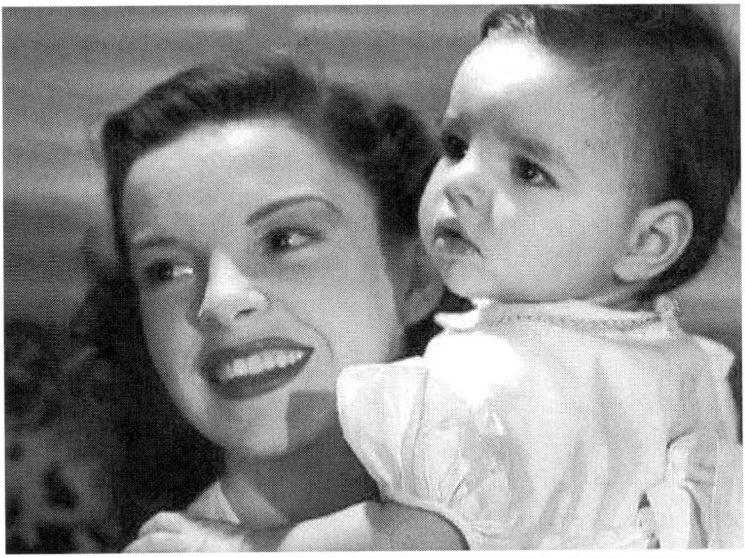

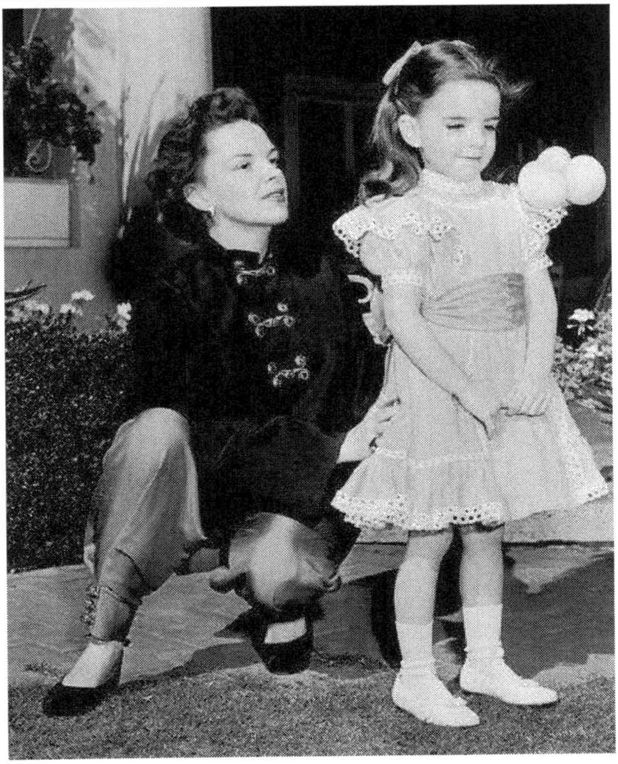

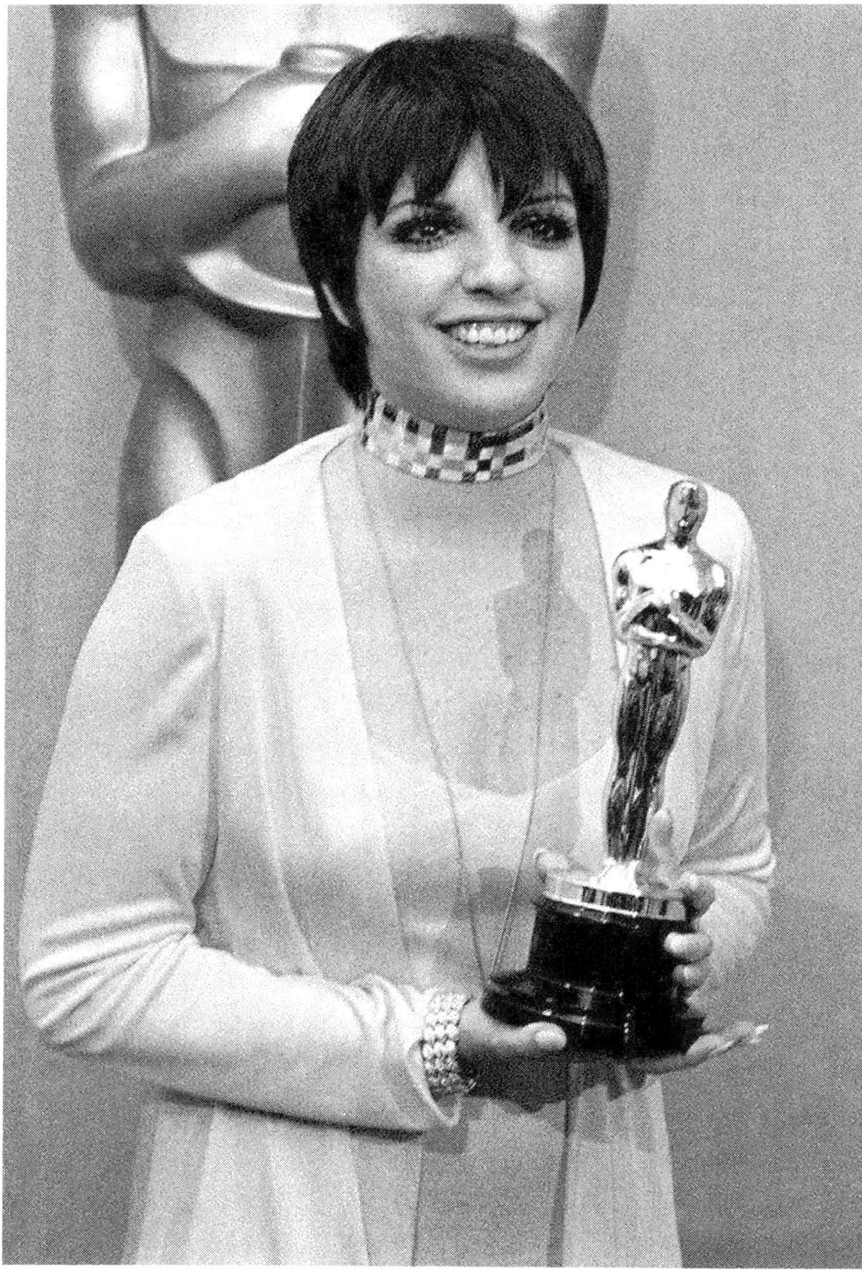

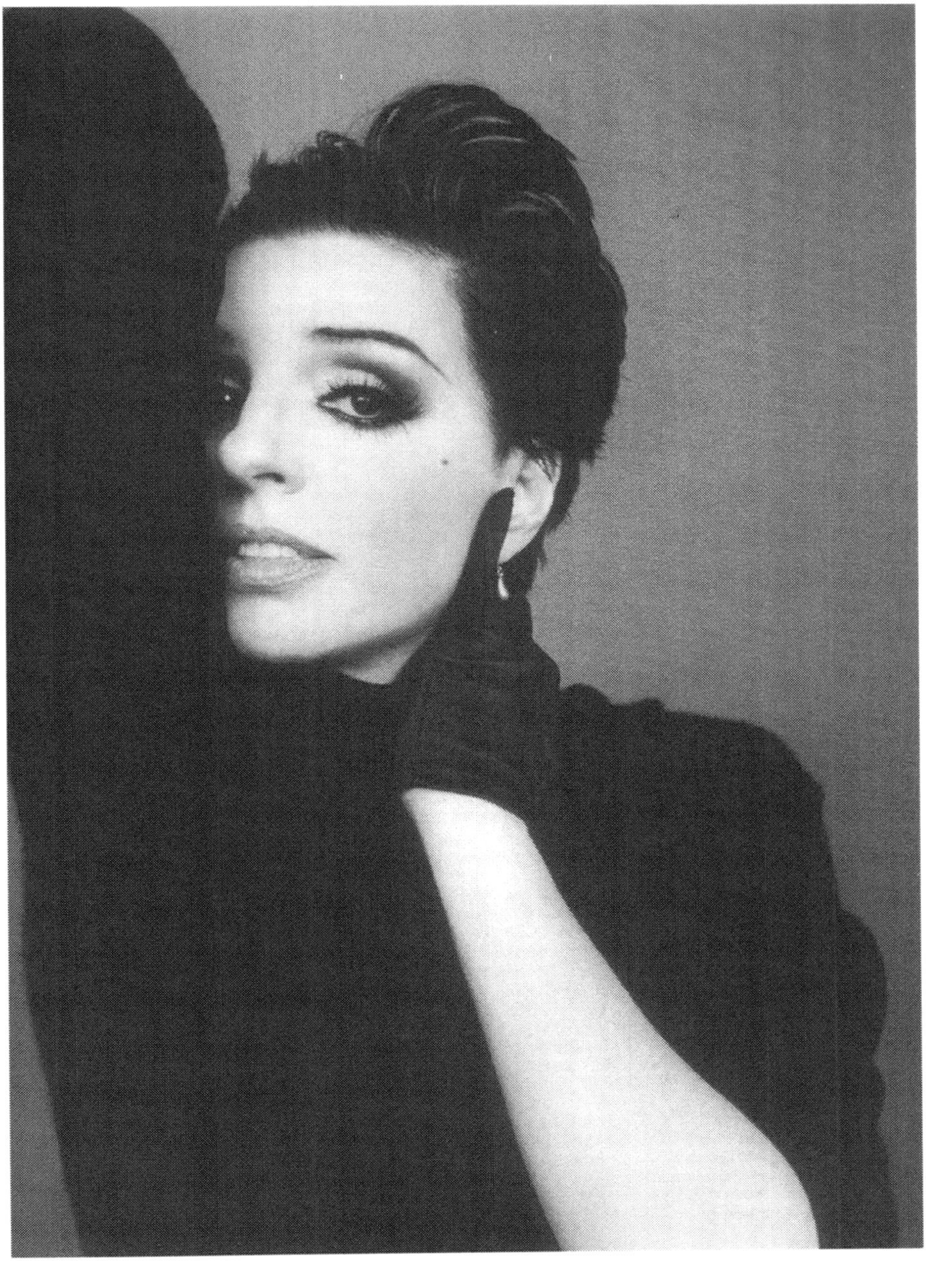

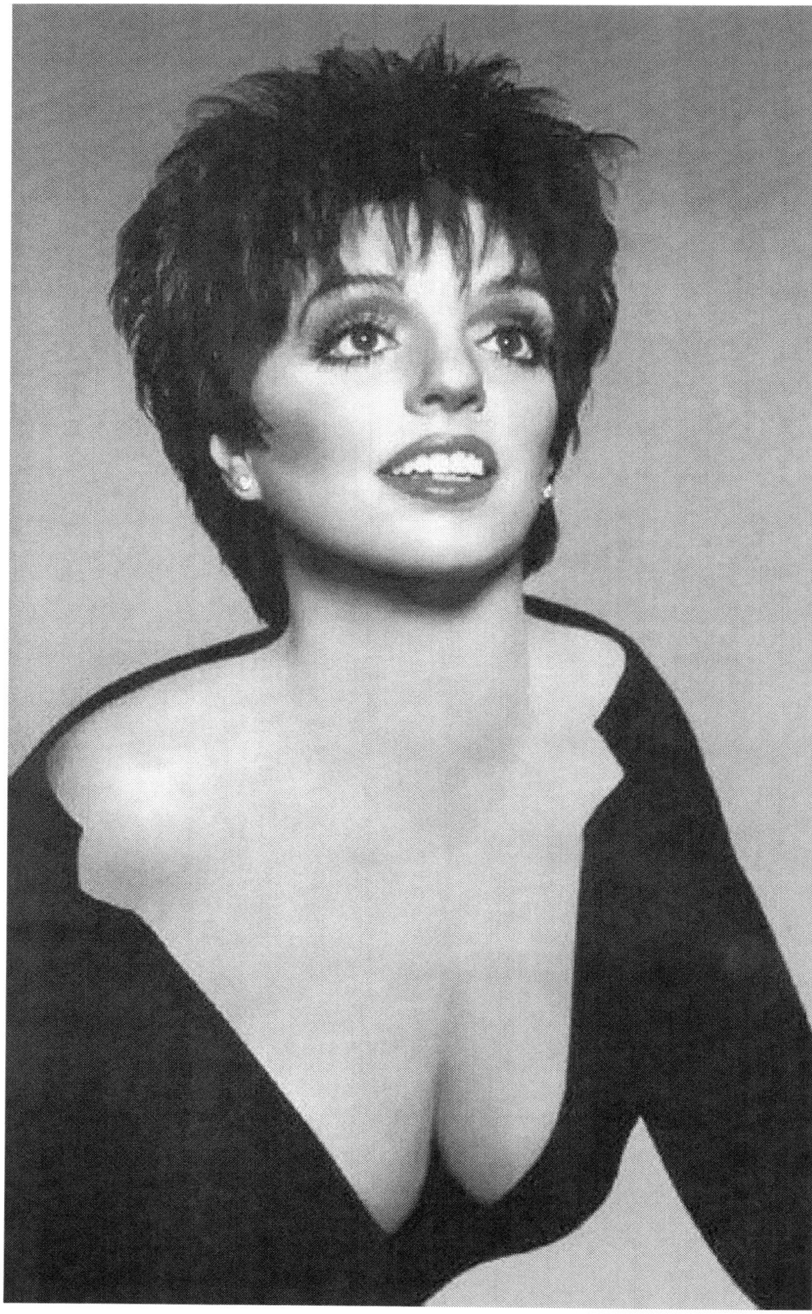

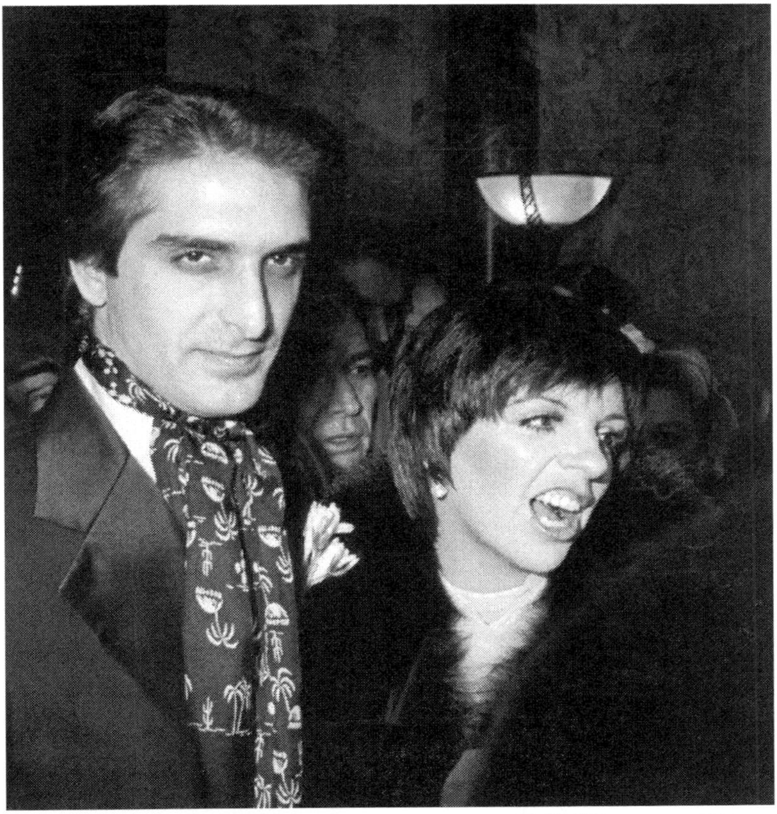

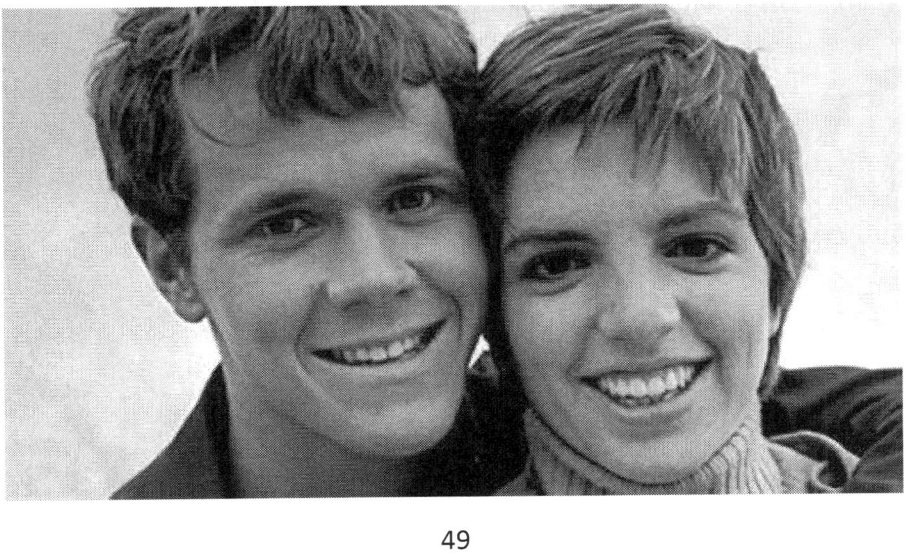

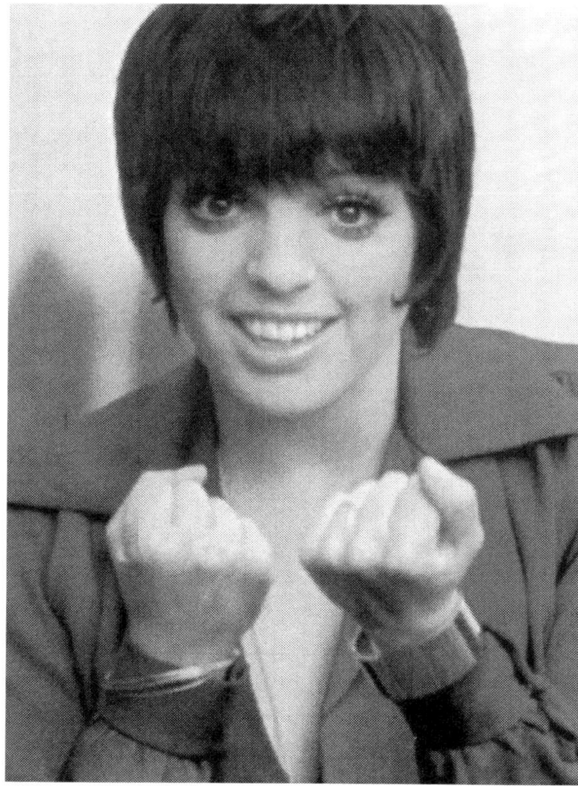

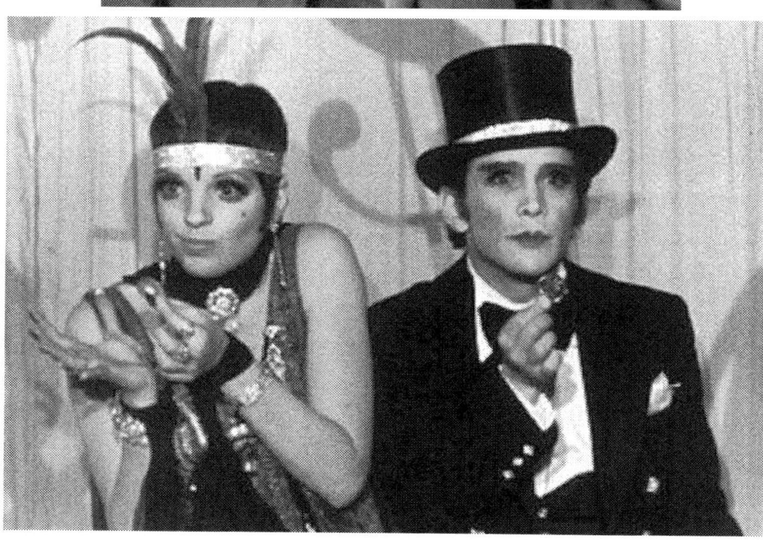

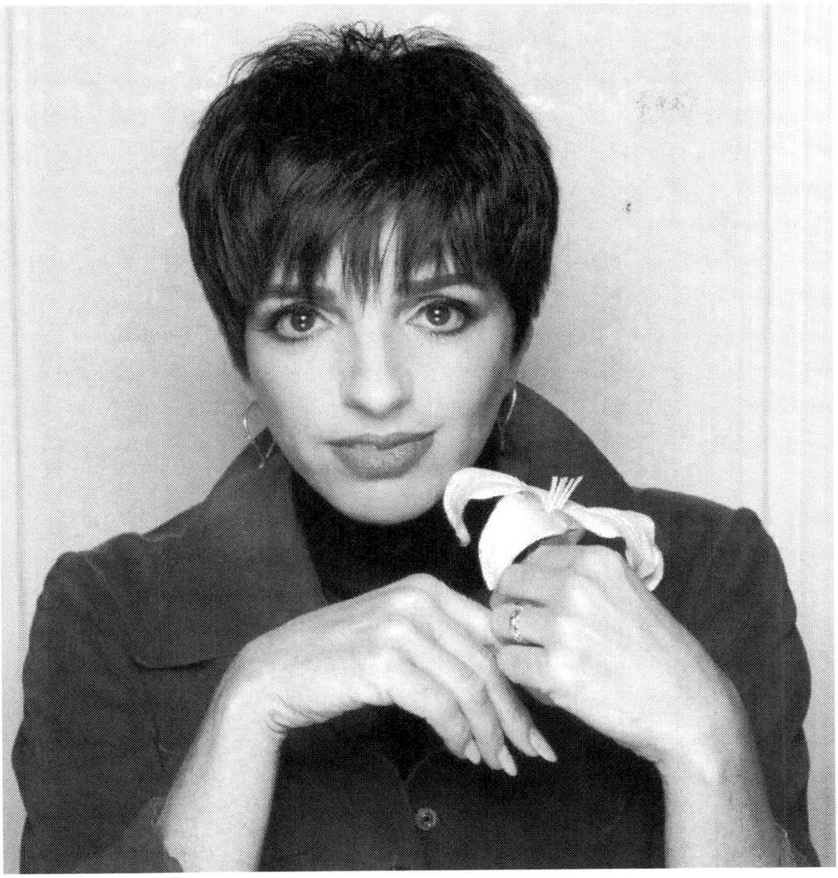

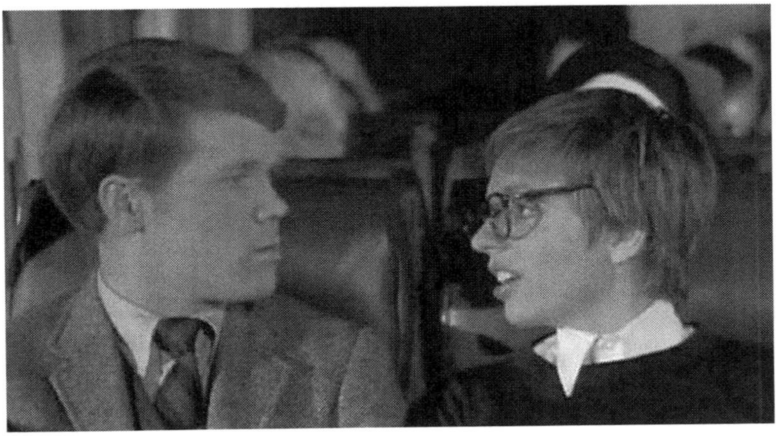

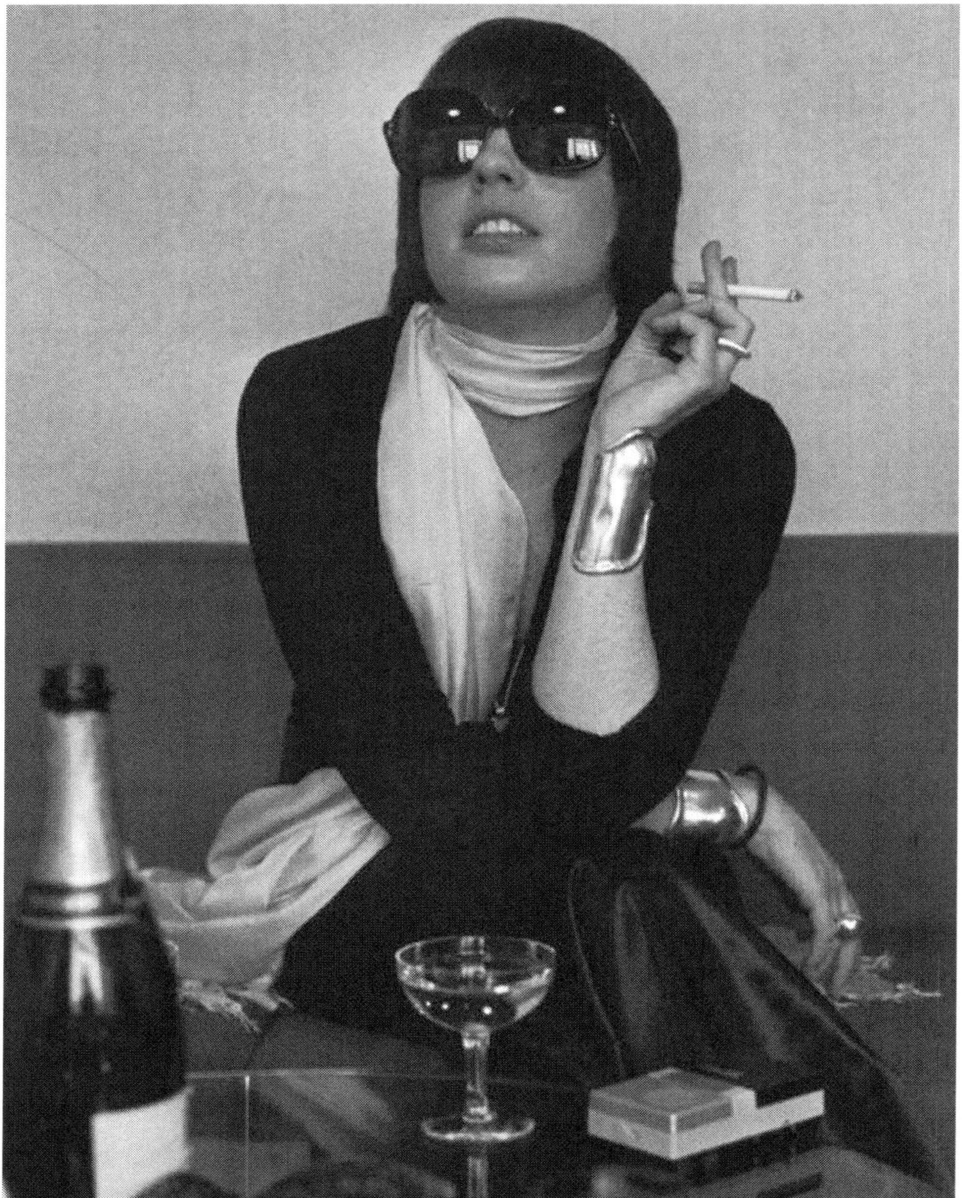

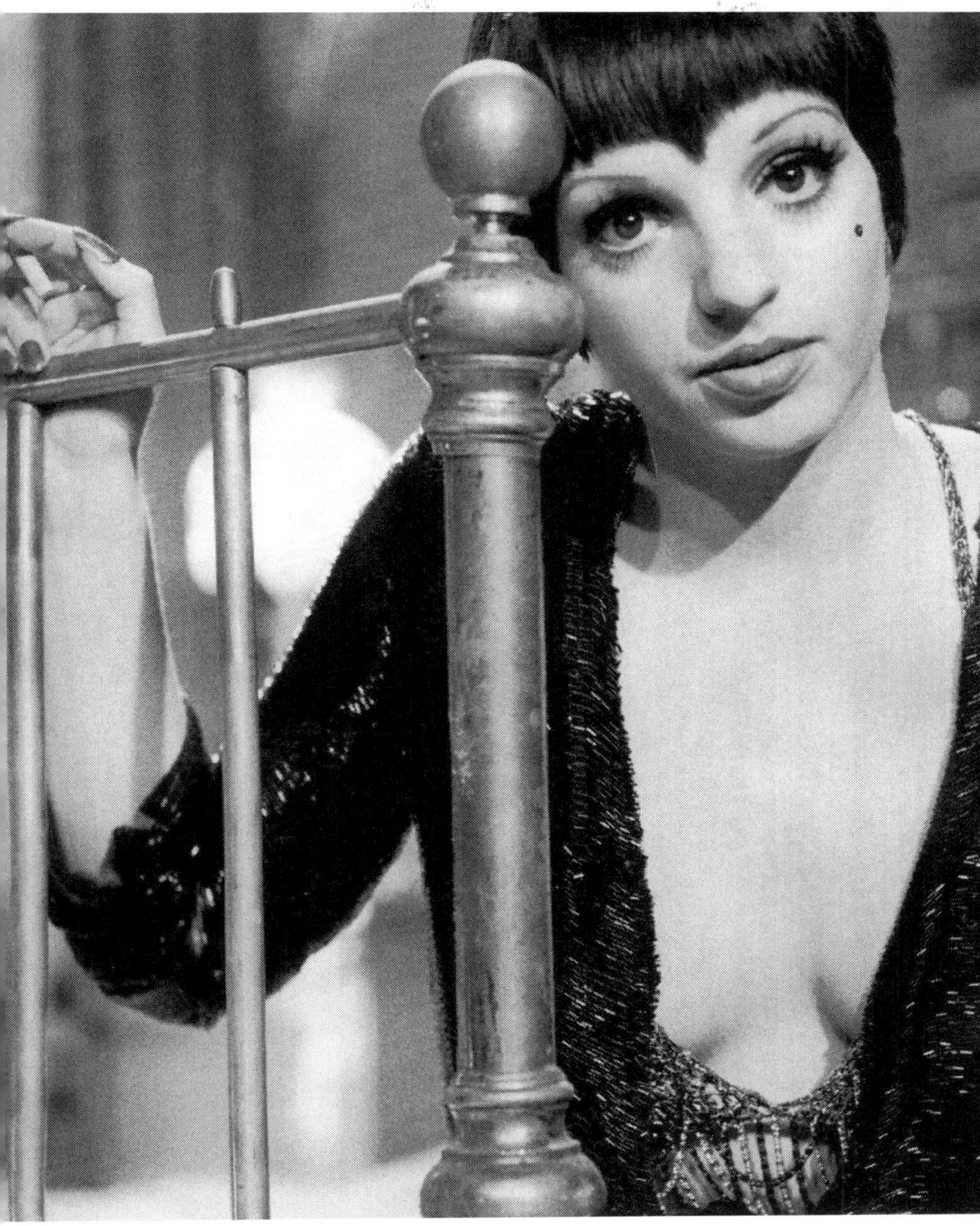

54

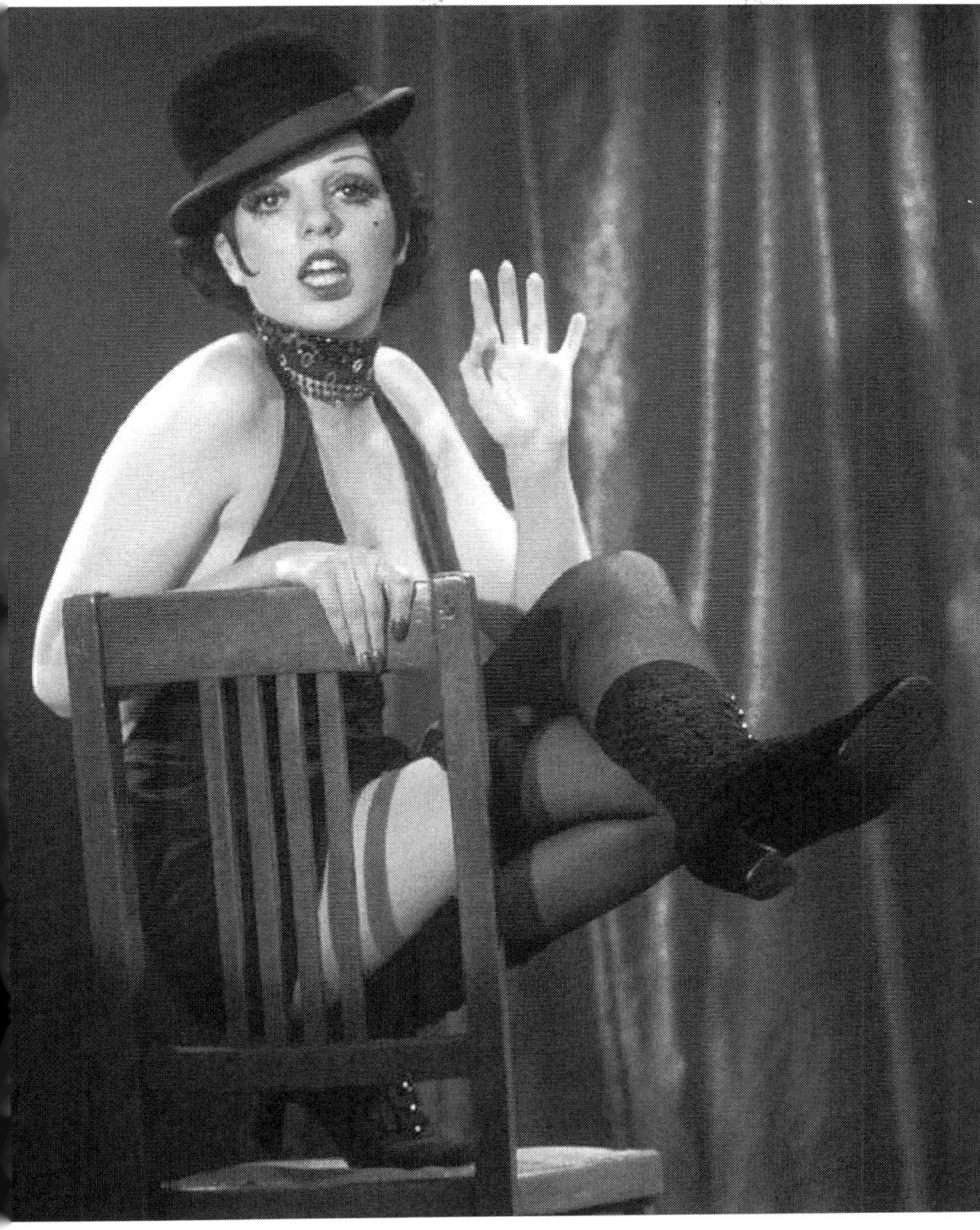

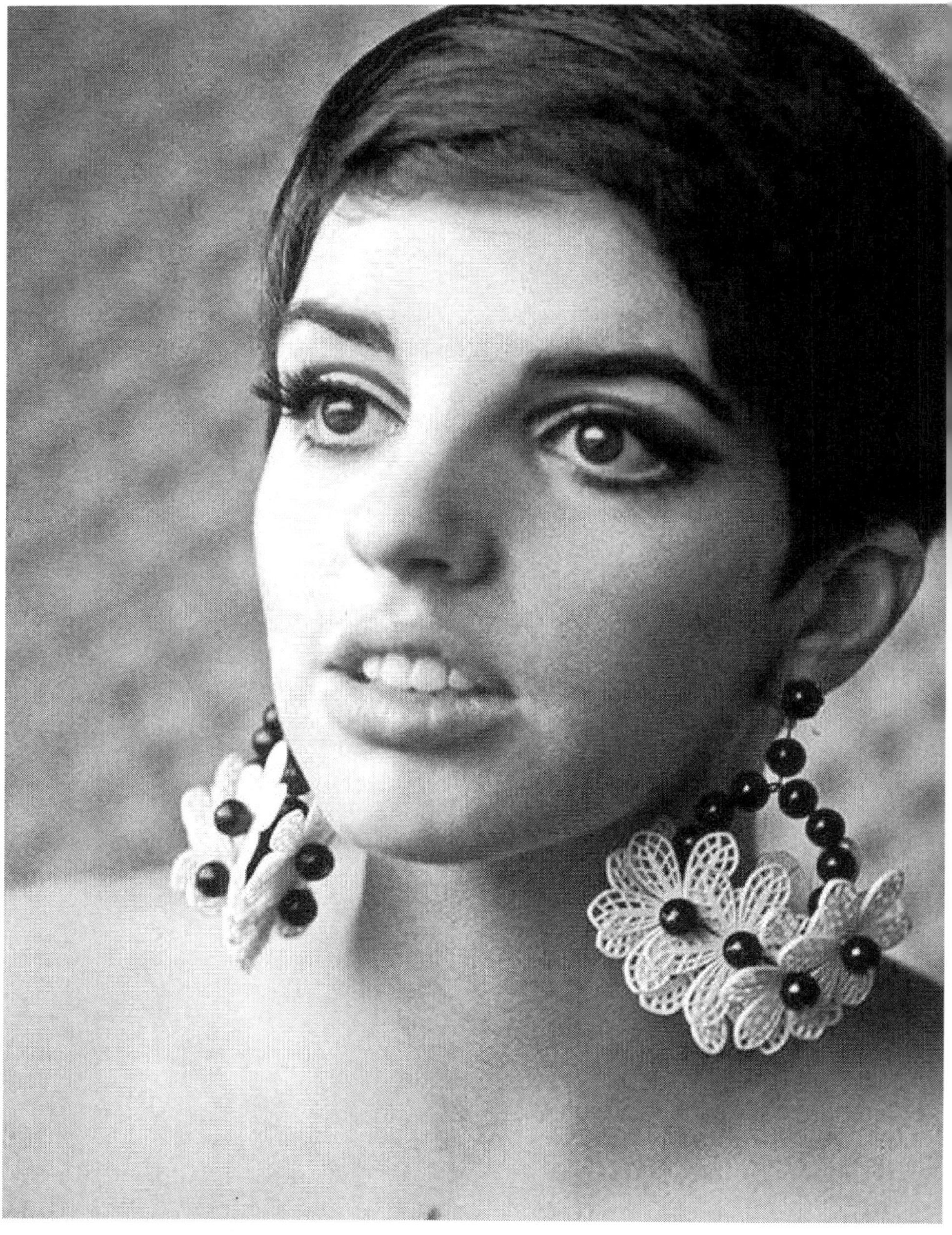

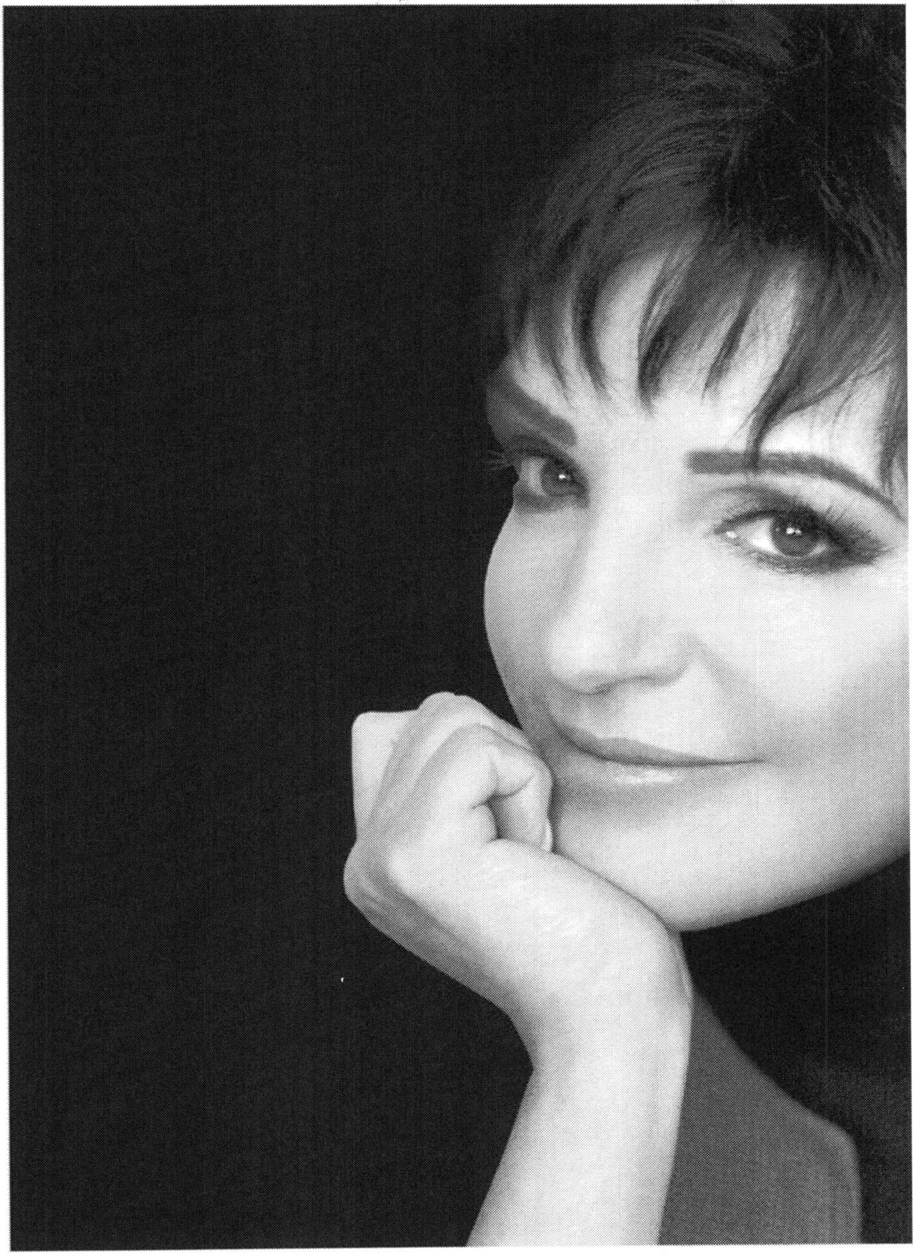

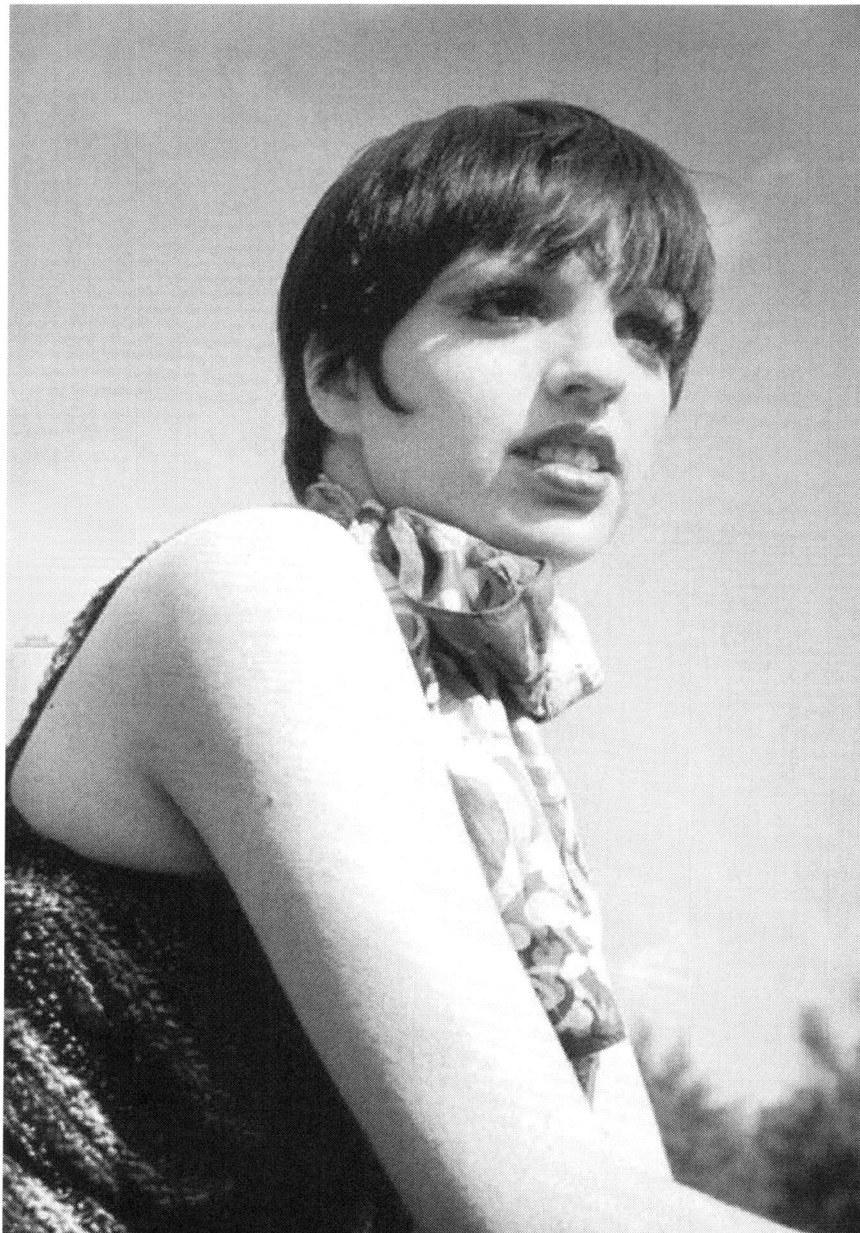

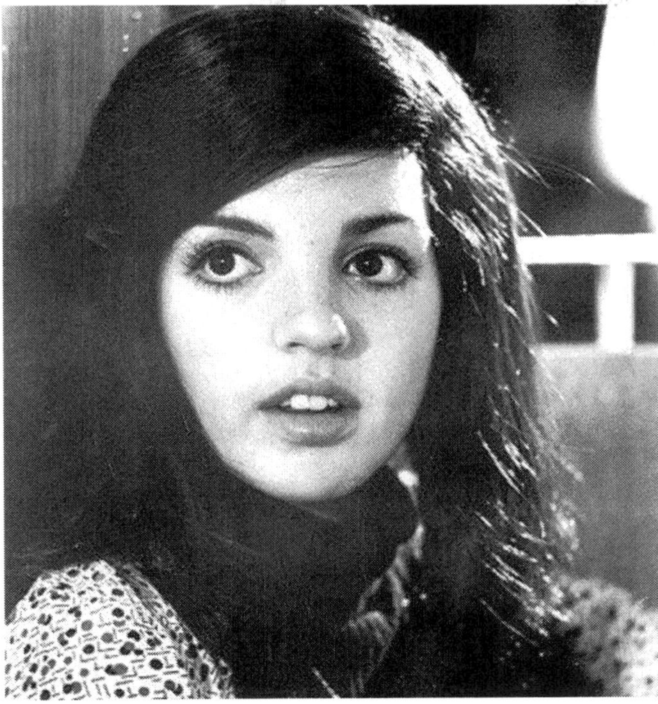

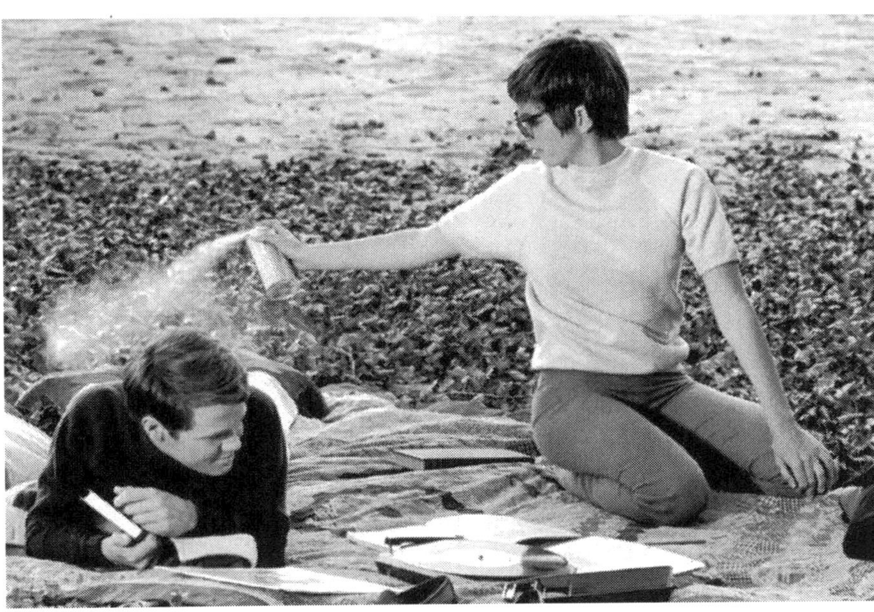

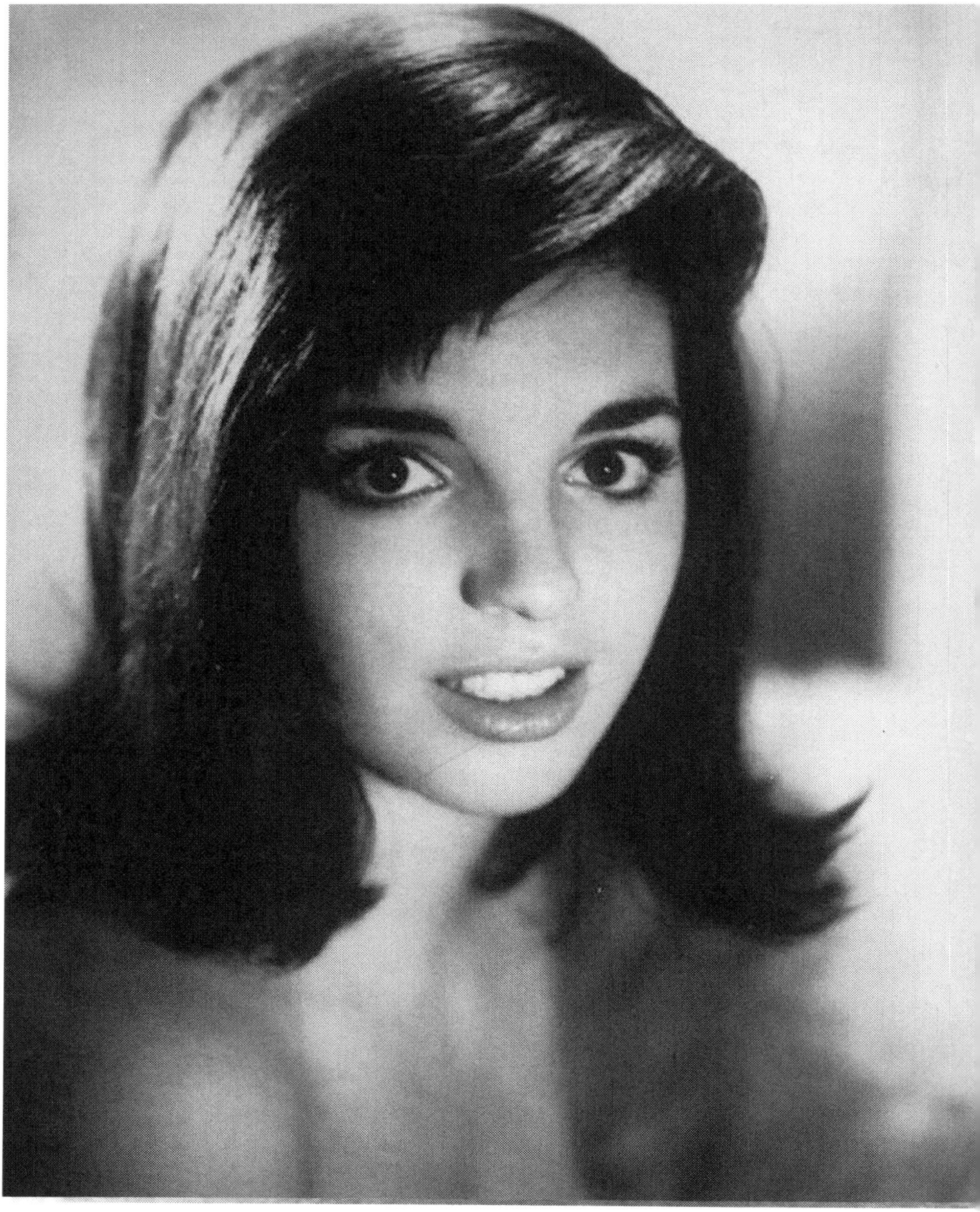

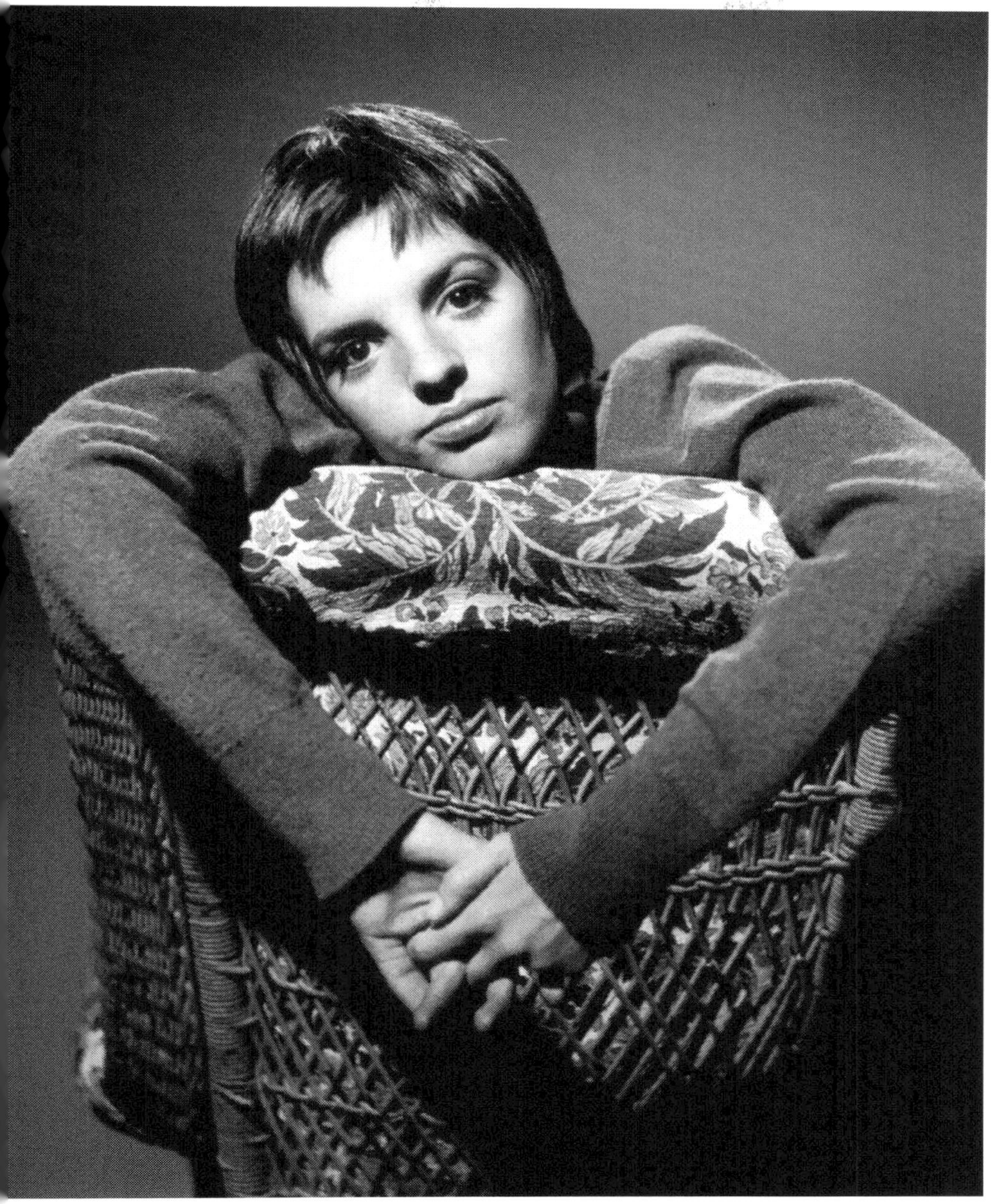

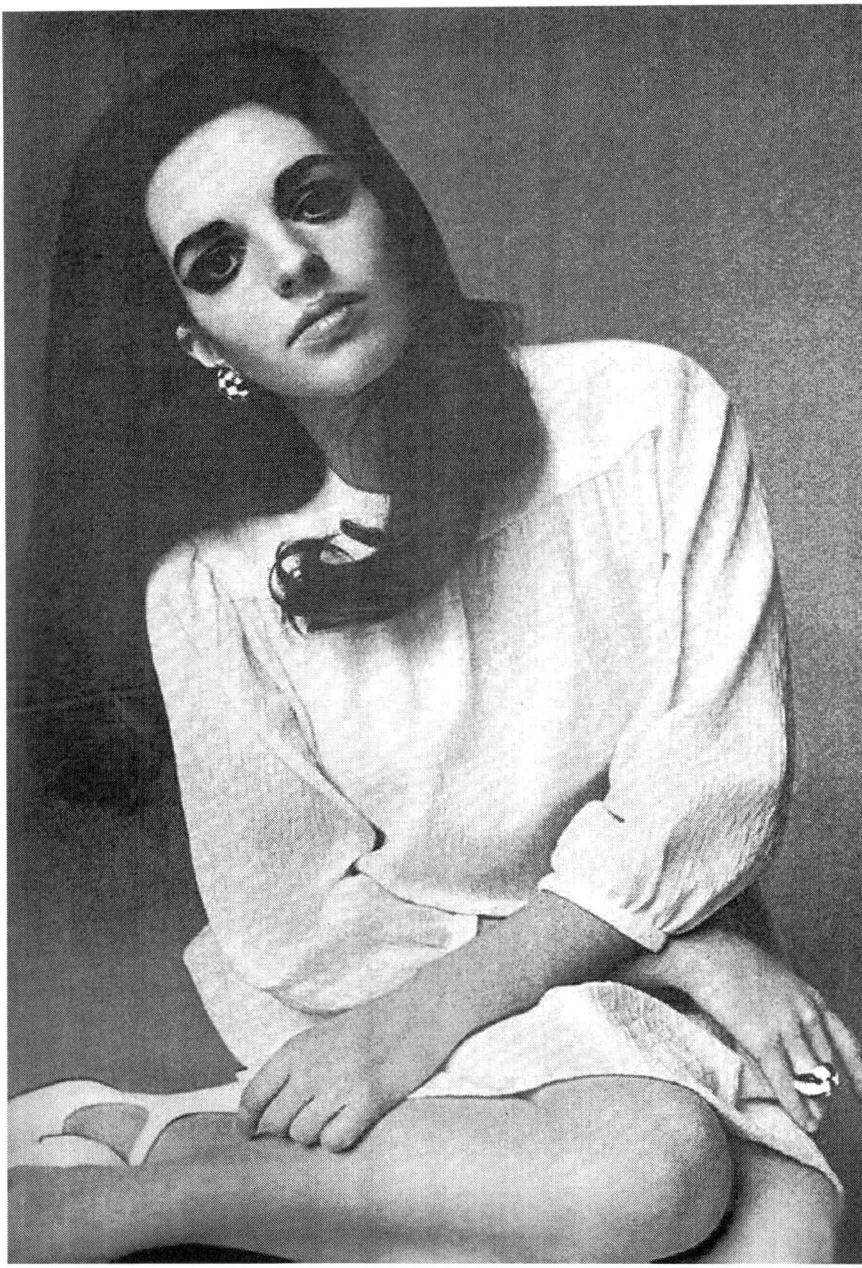

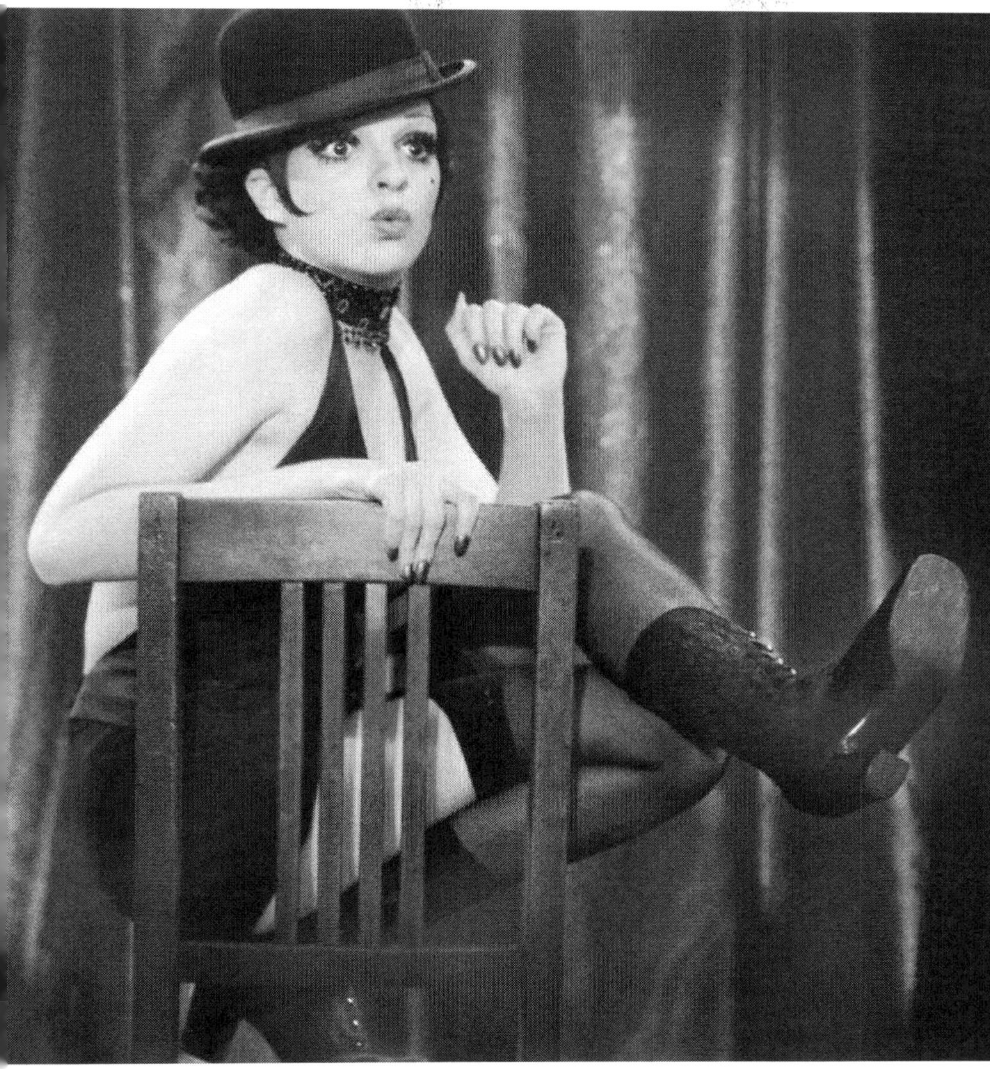

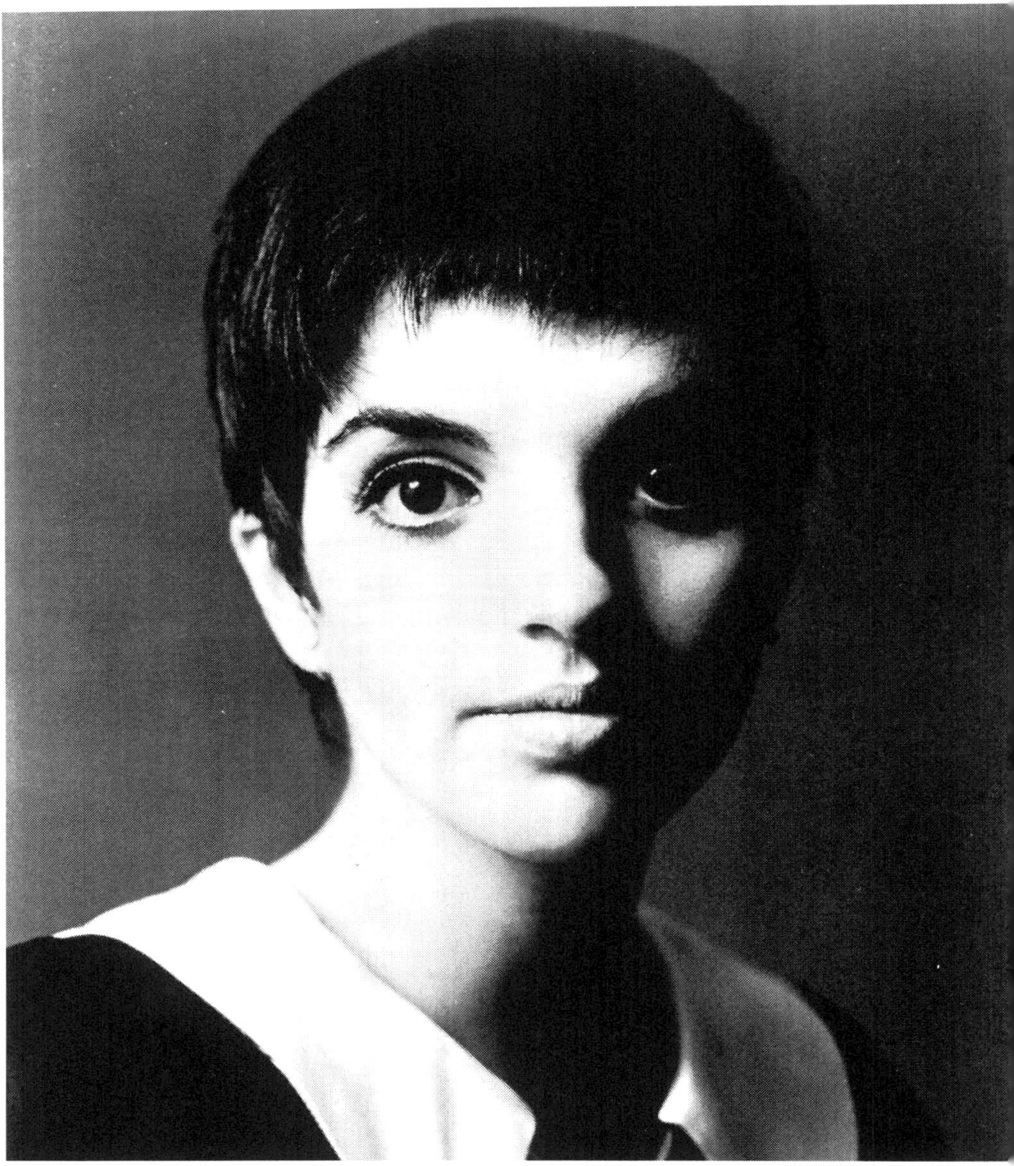

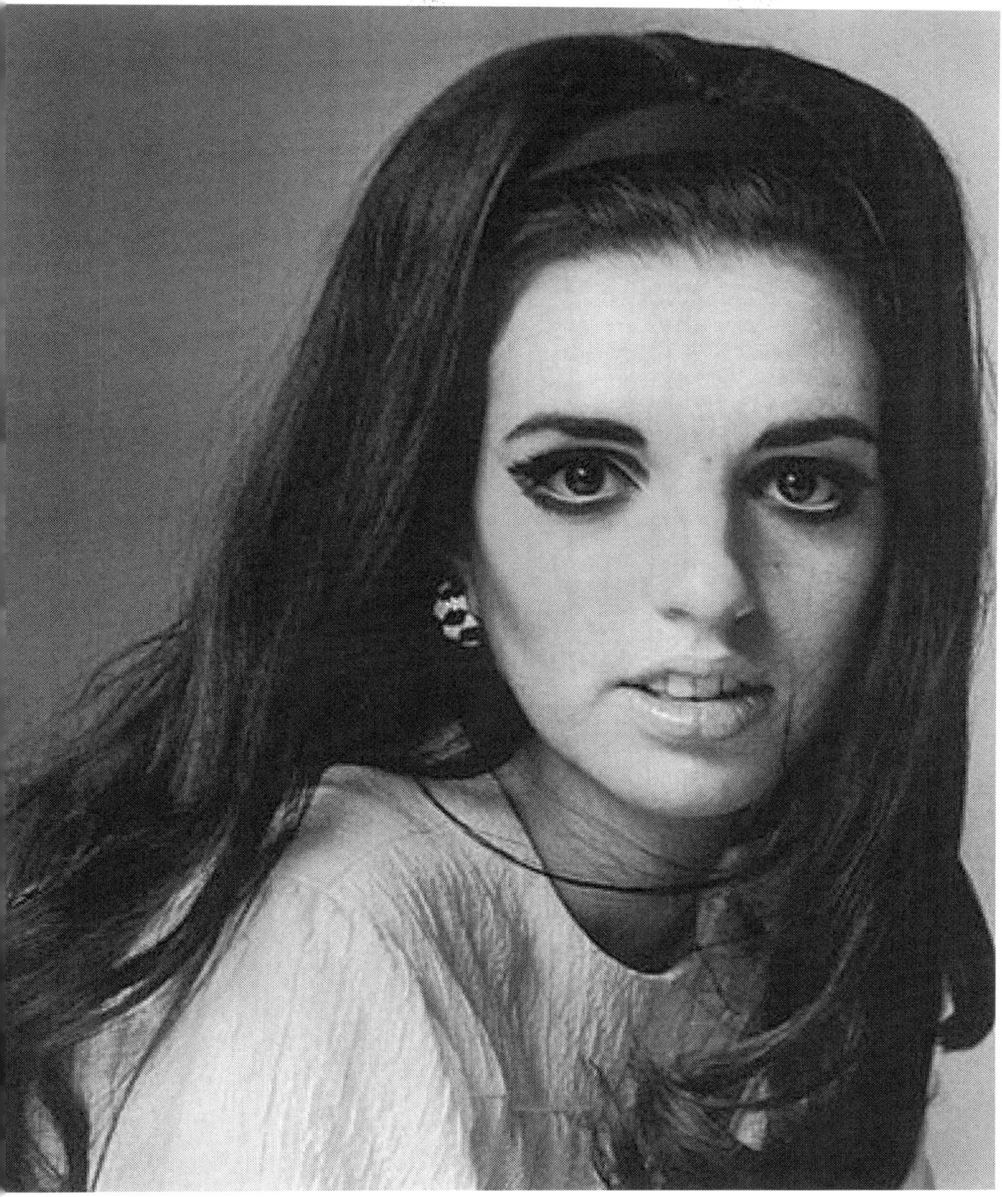

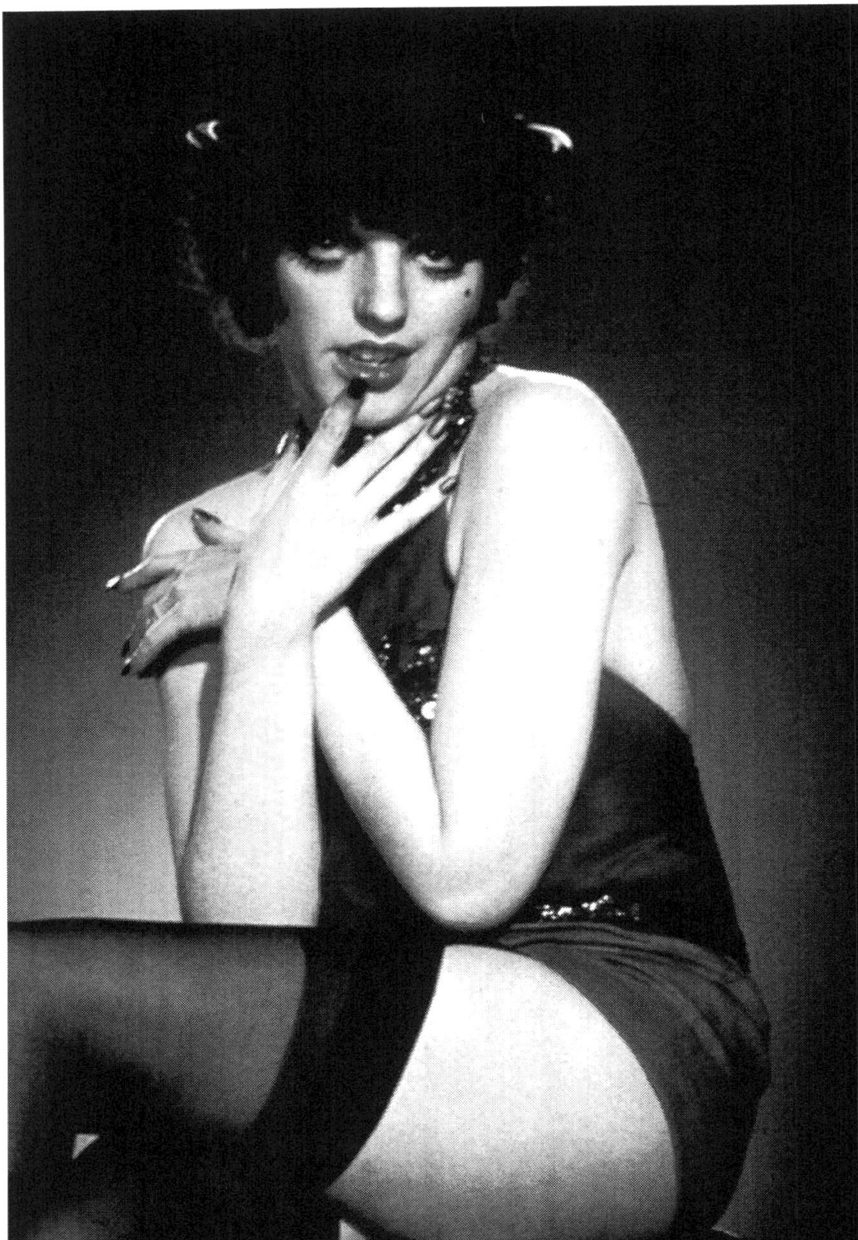

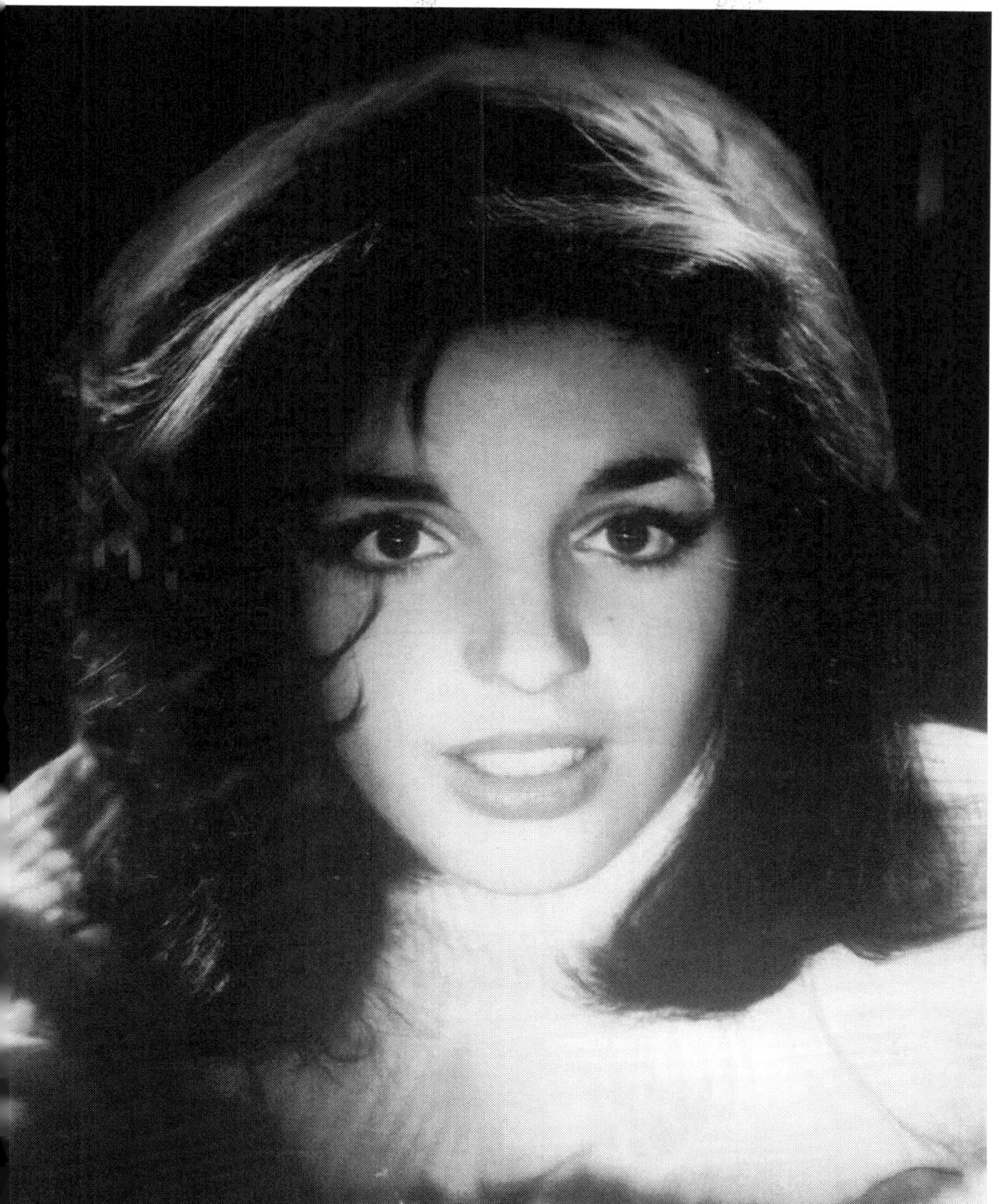

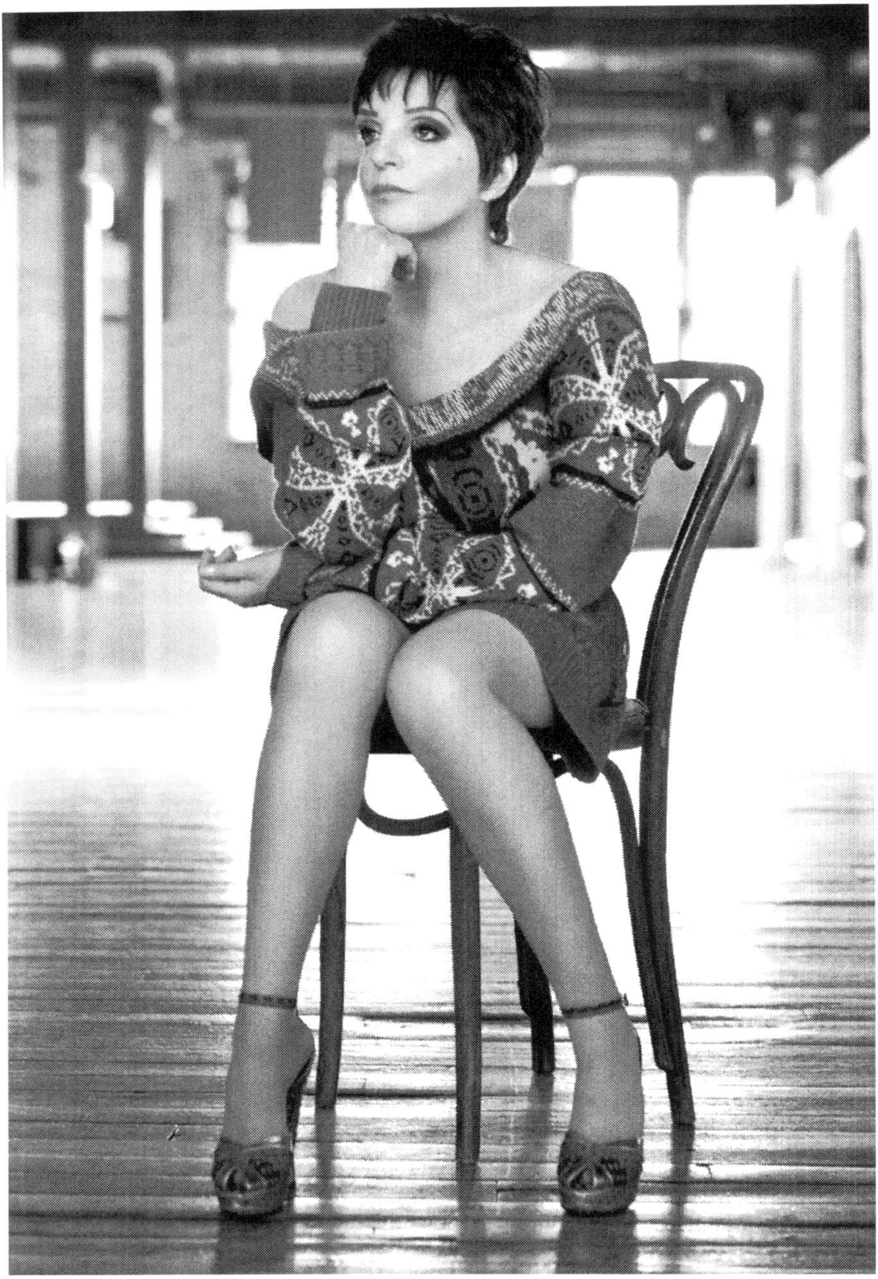

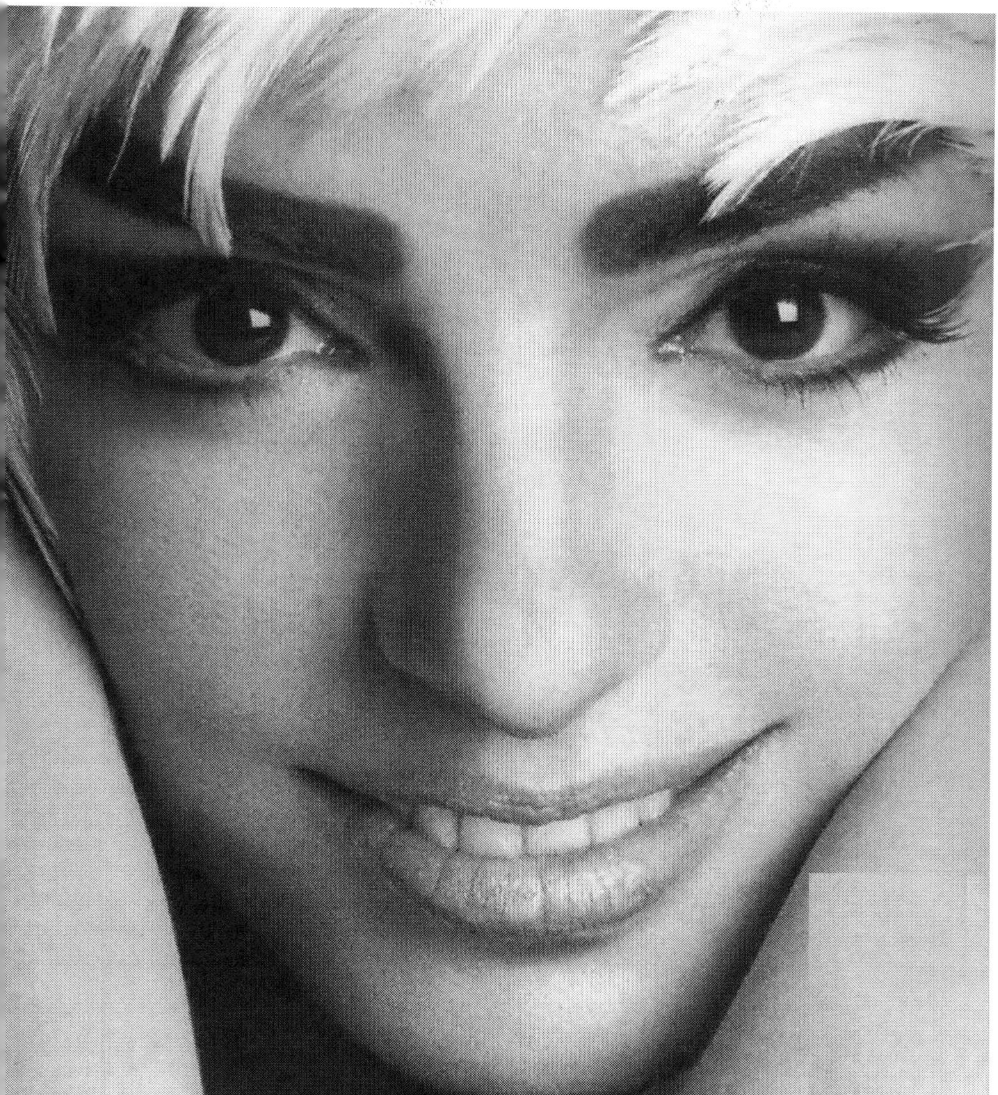

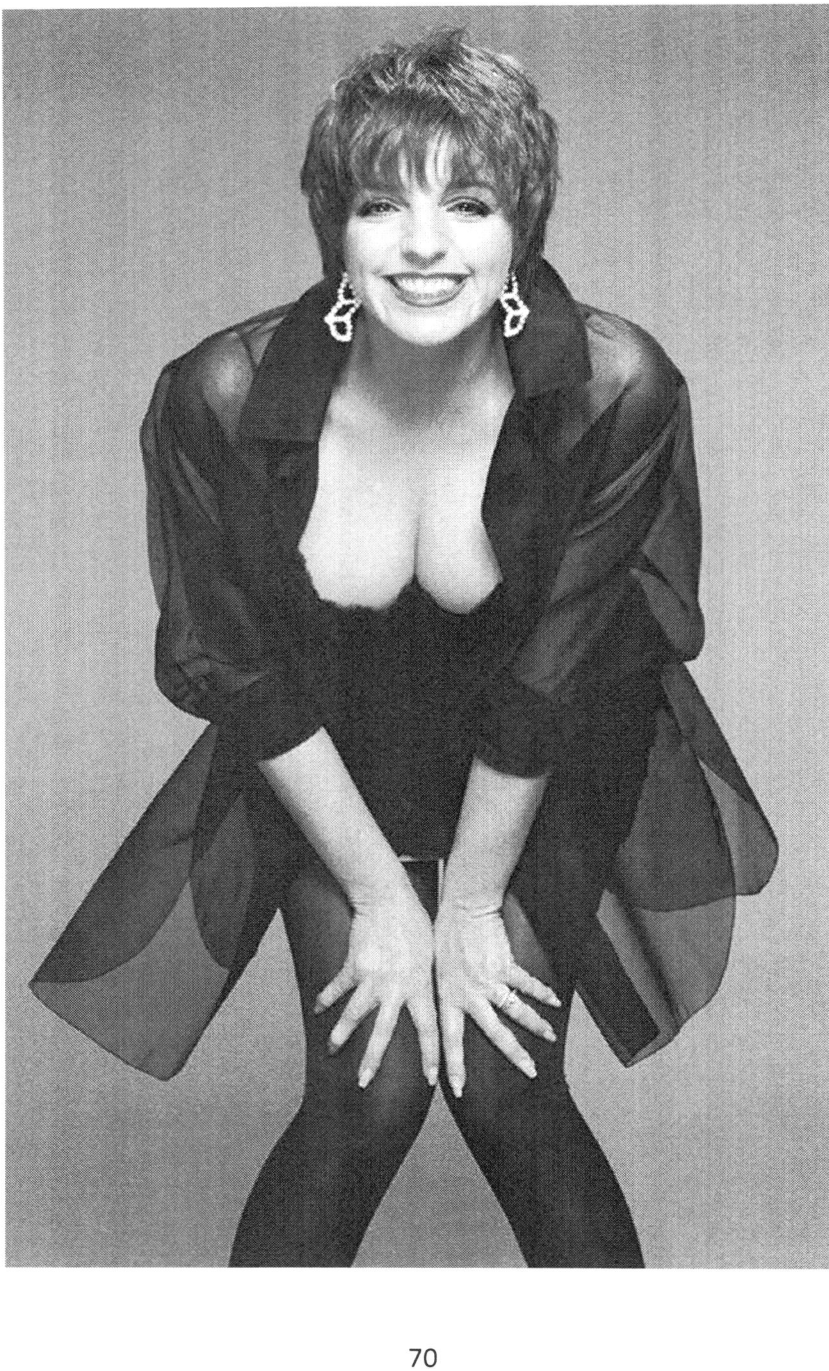

71

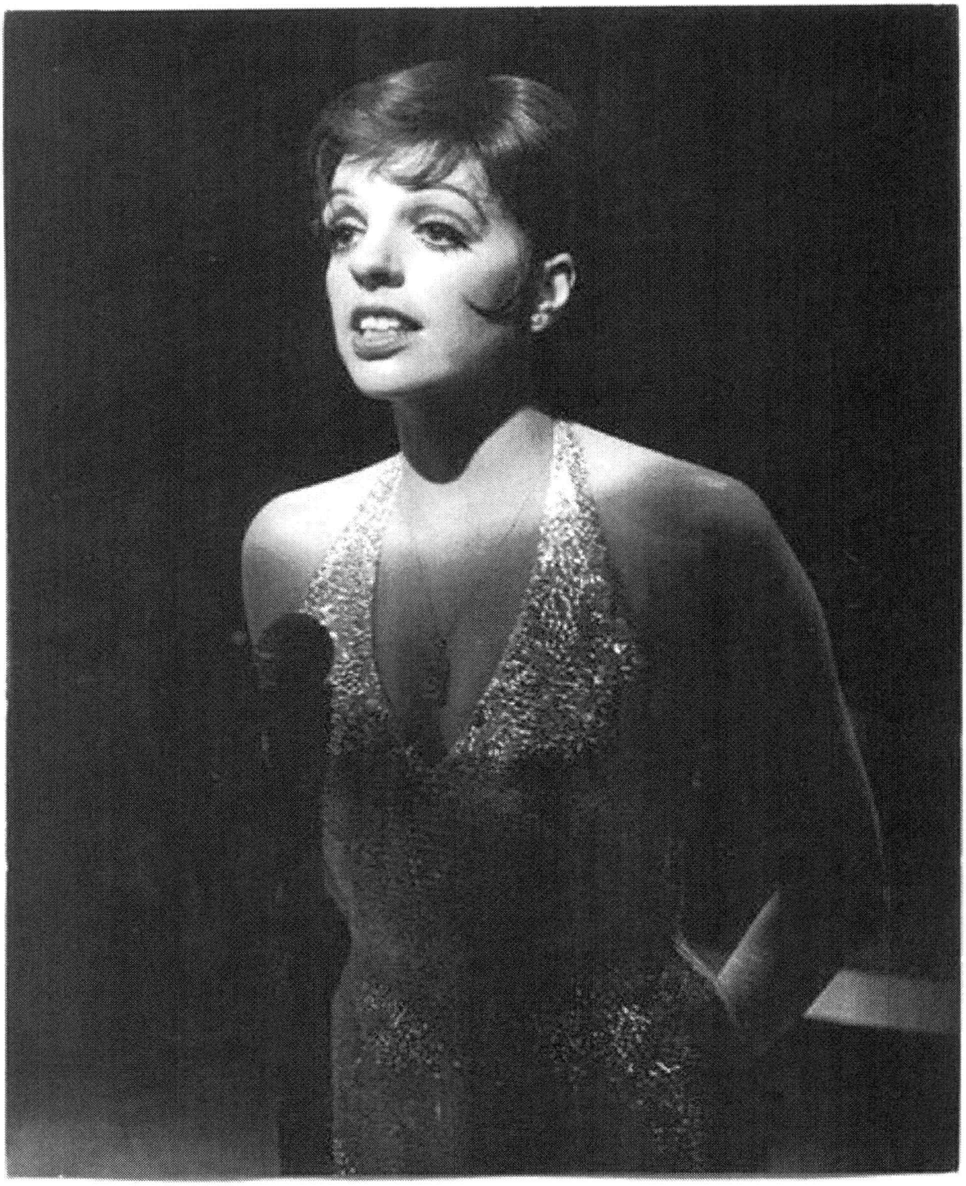

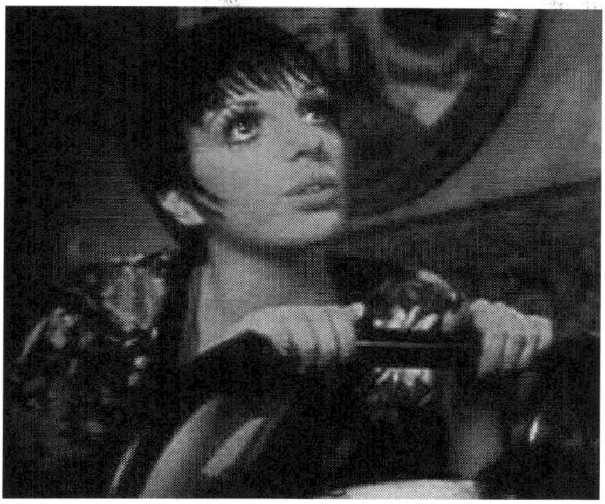

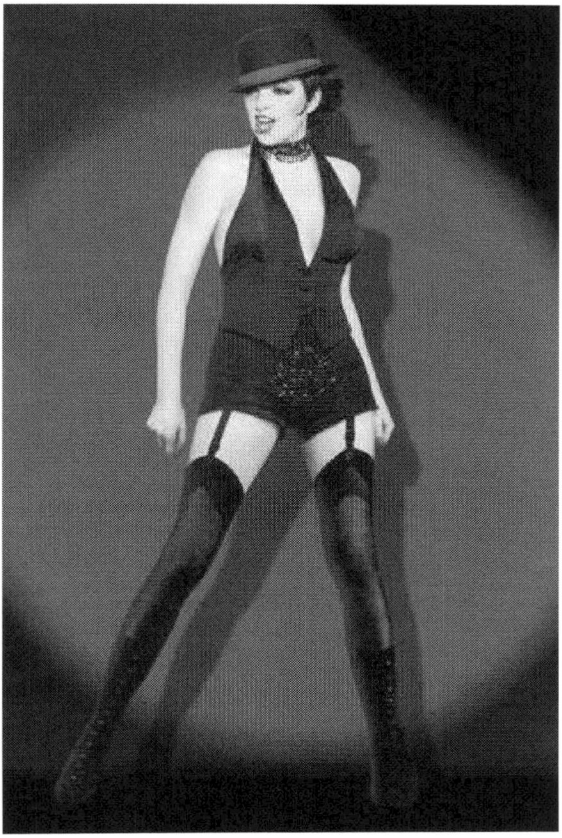

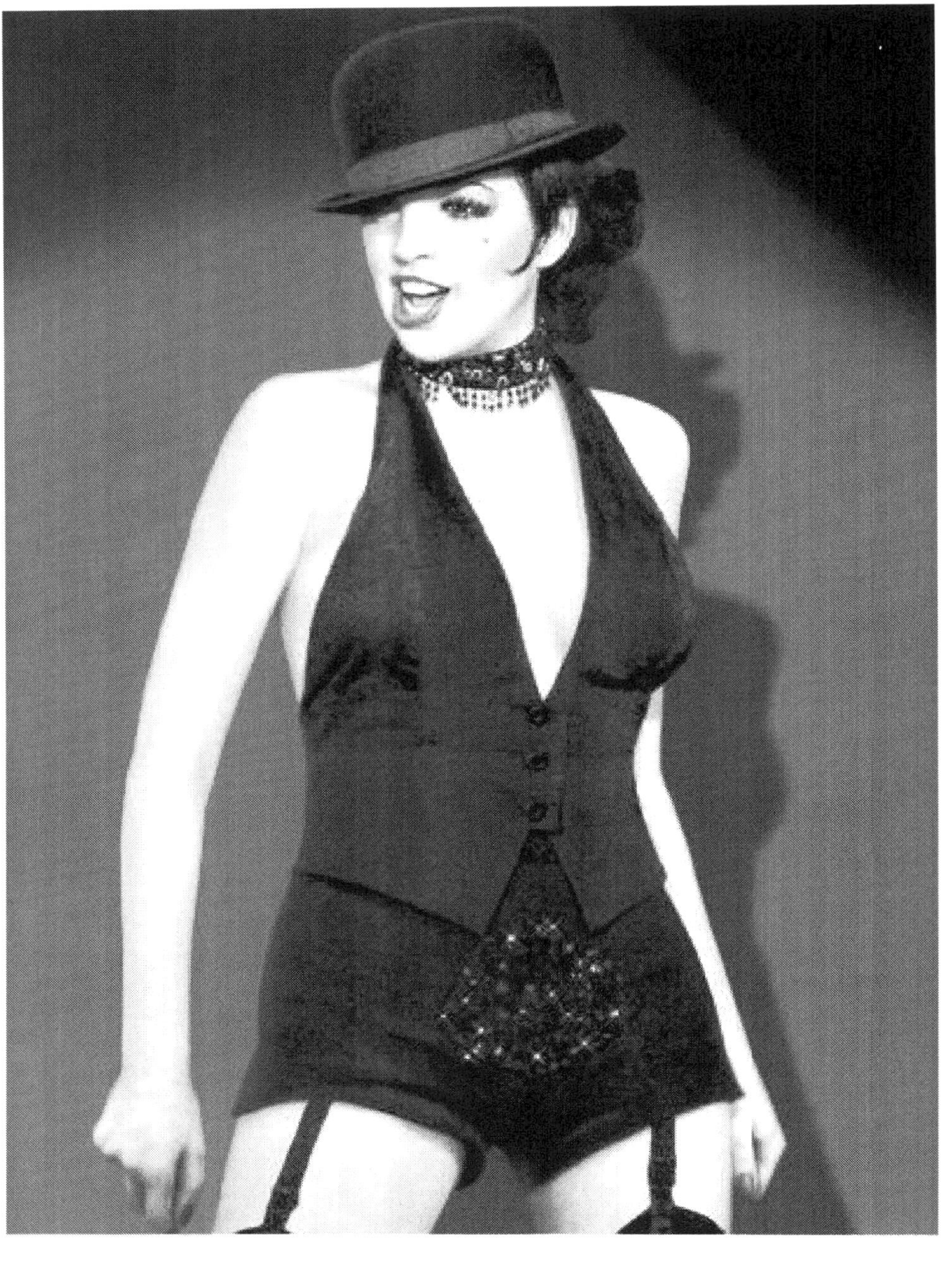

75

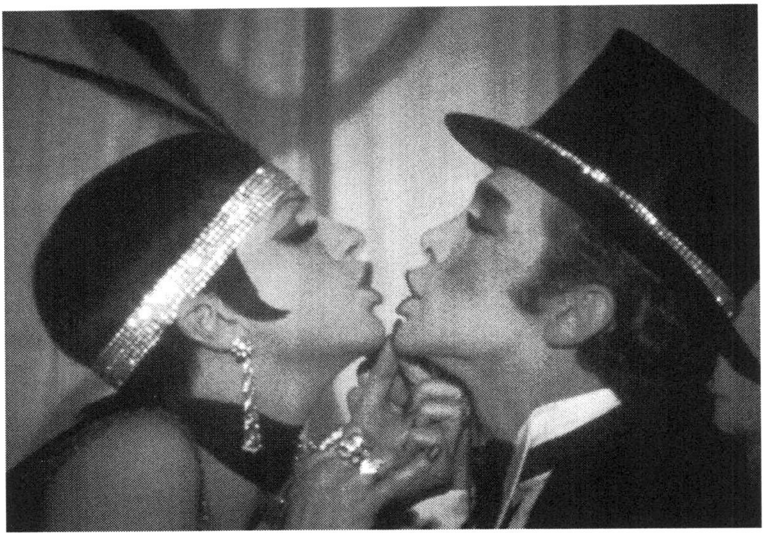

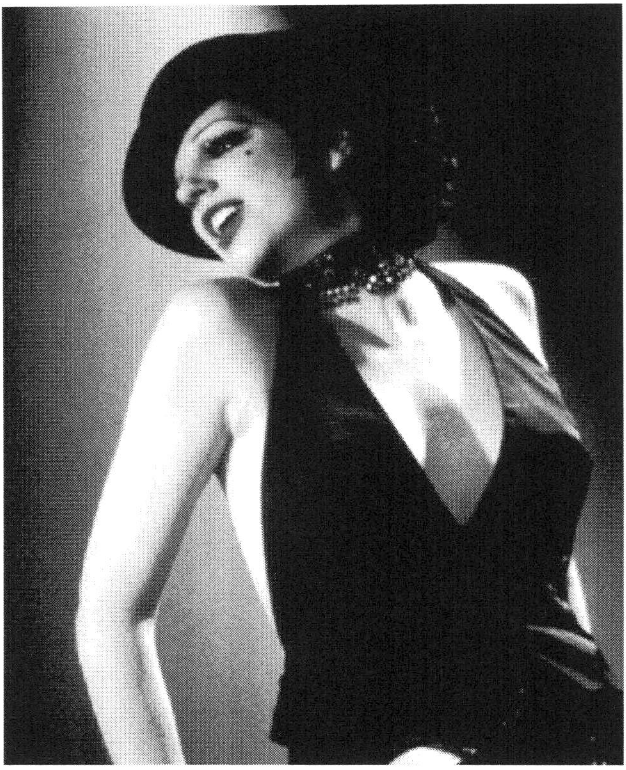

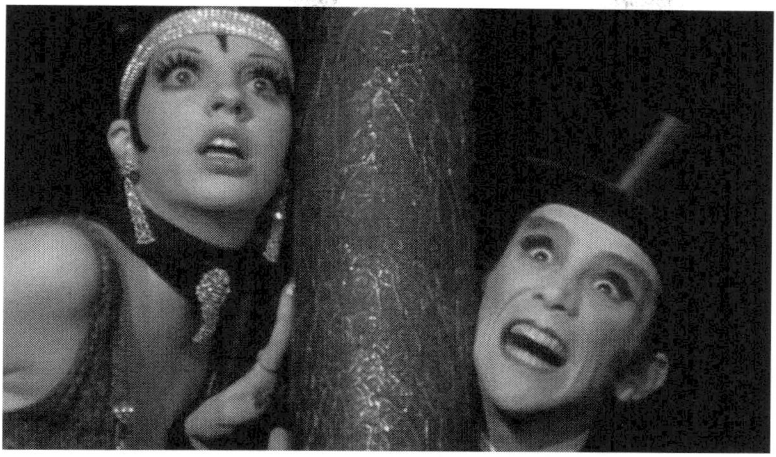

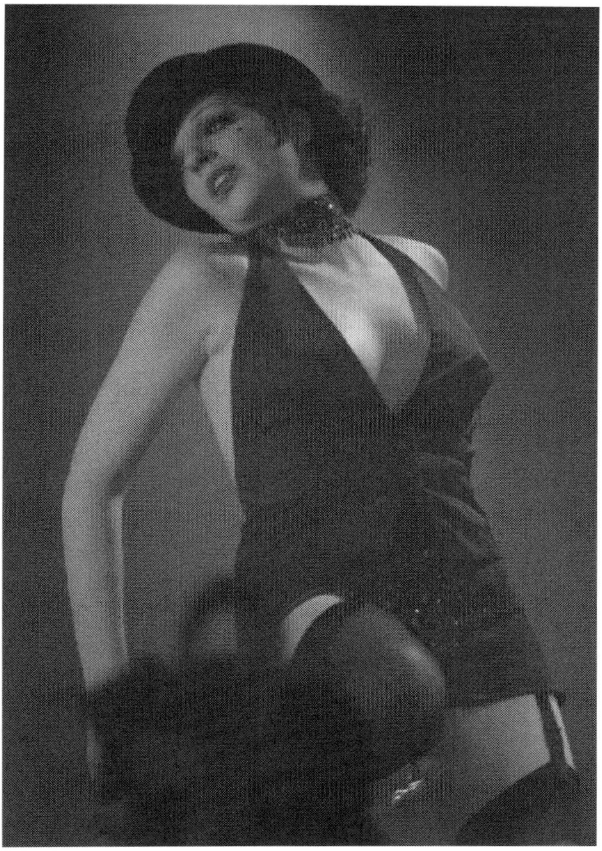

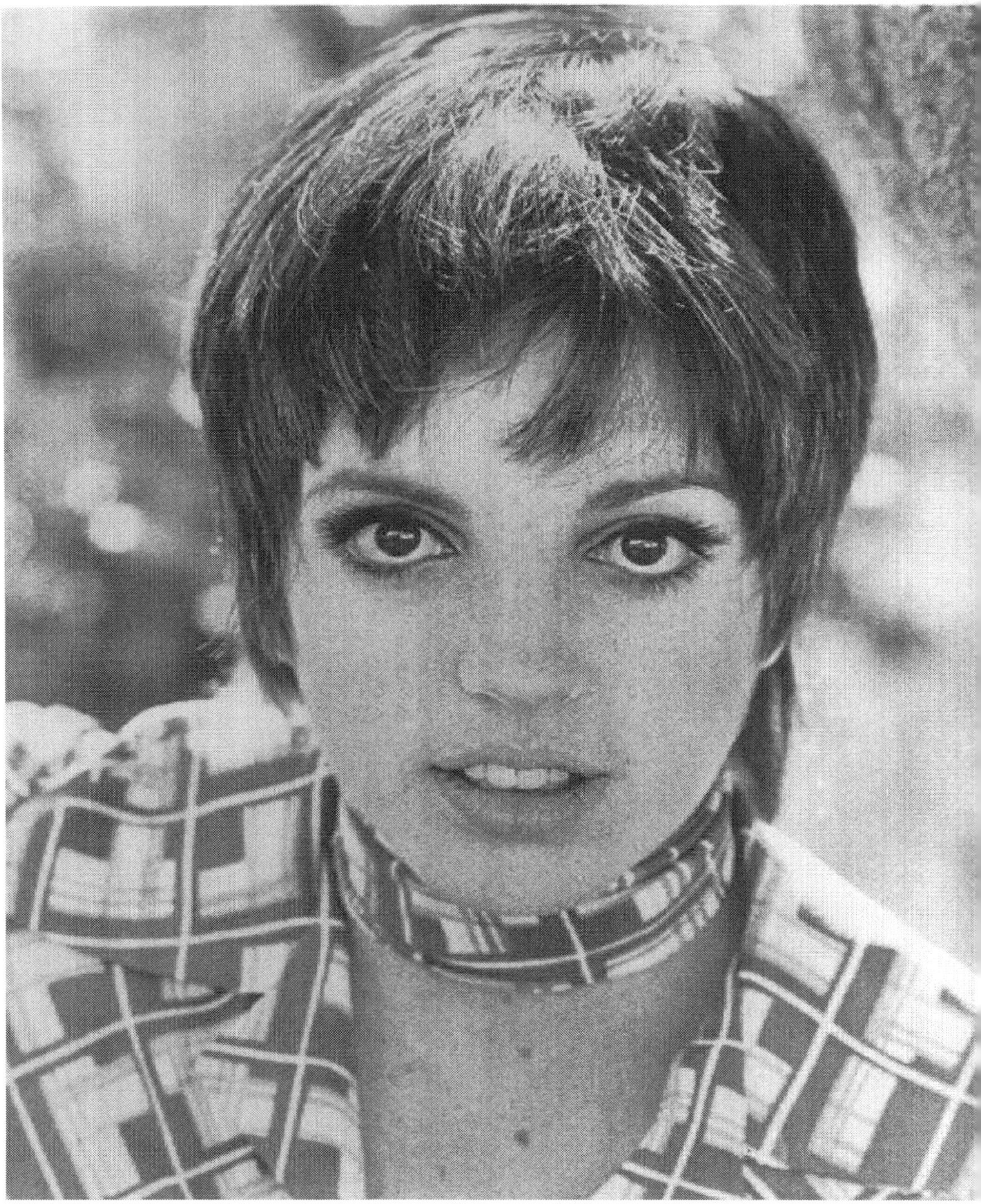

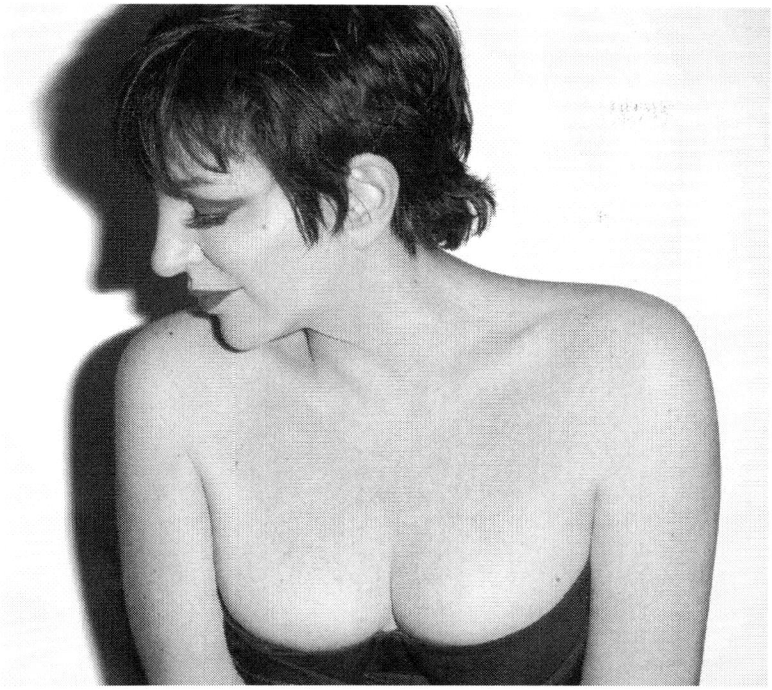

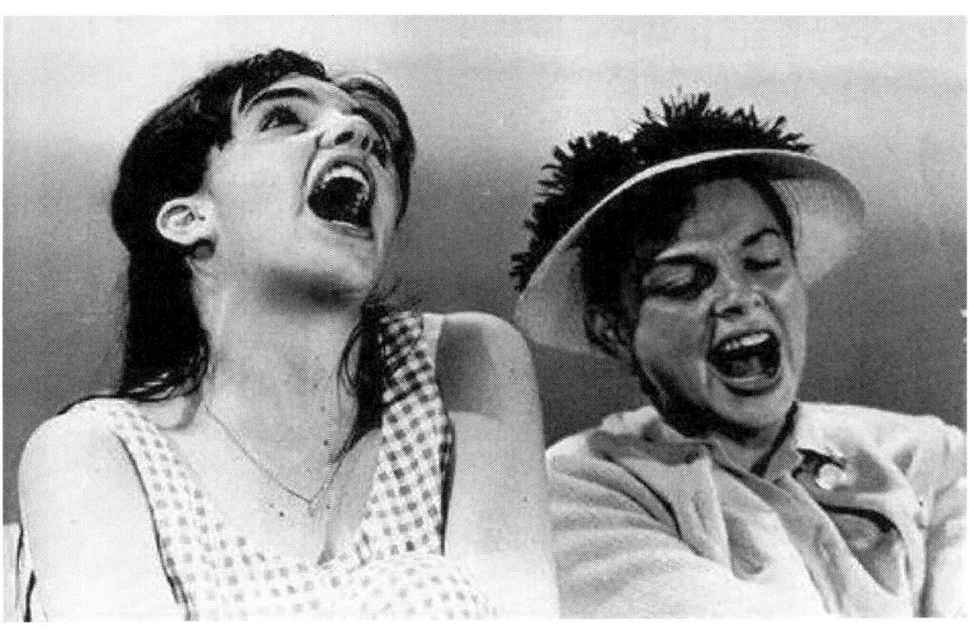

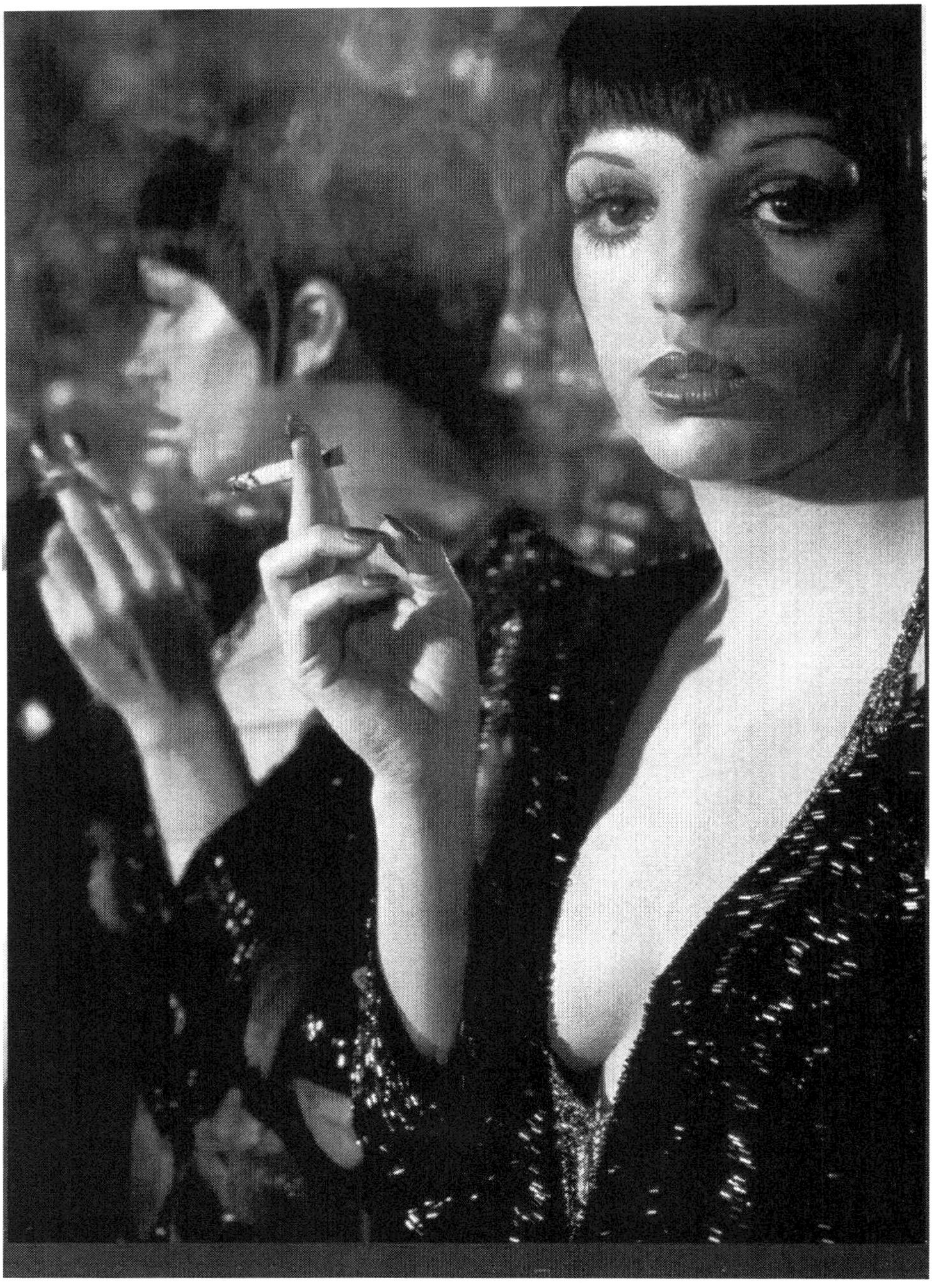

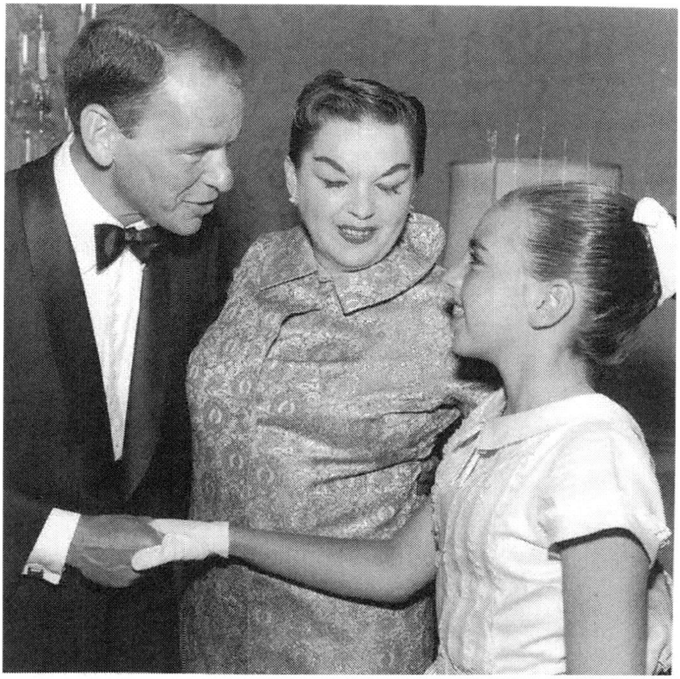

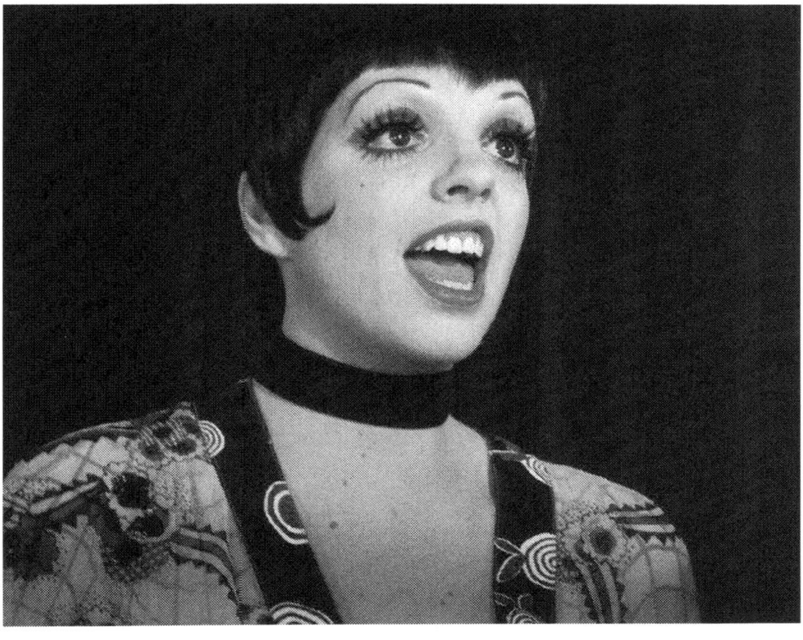

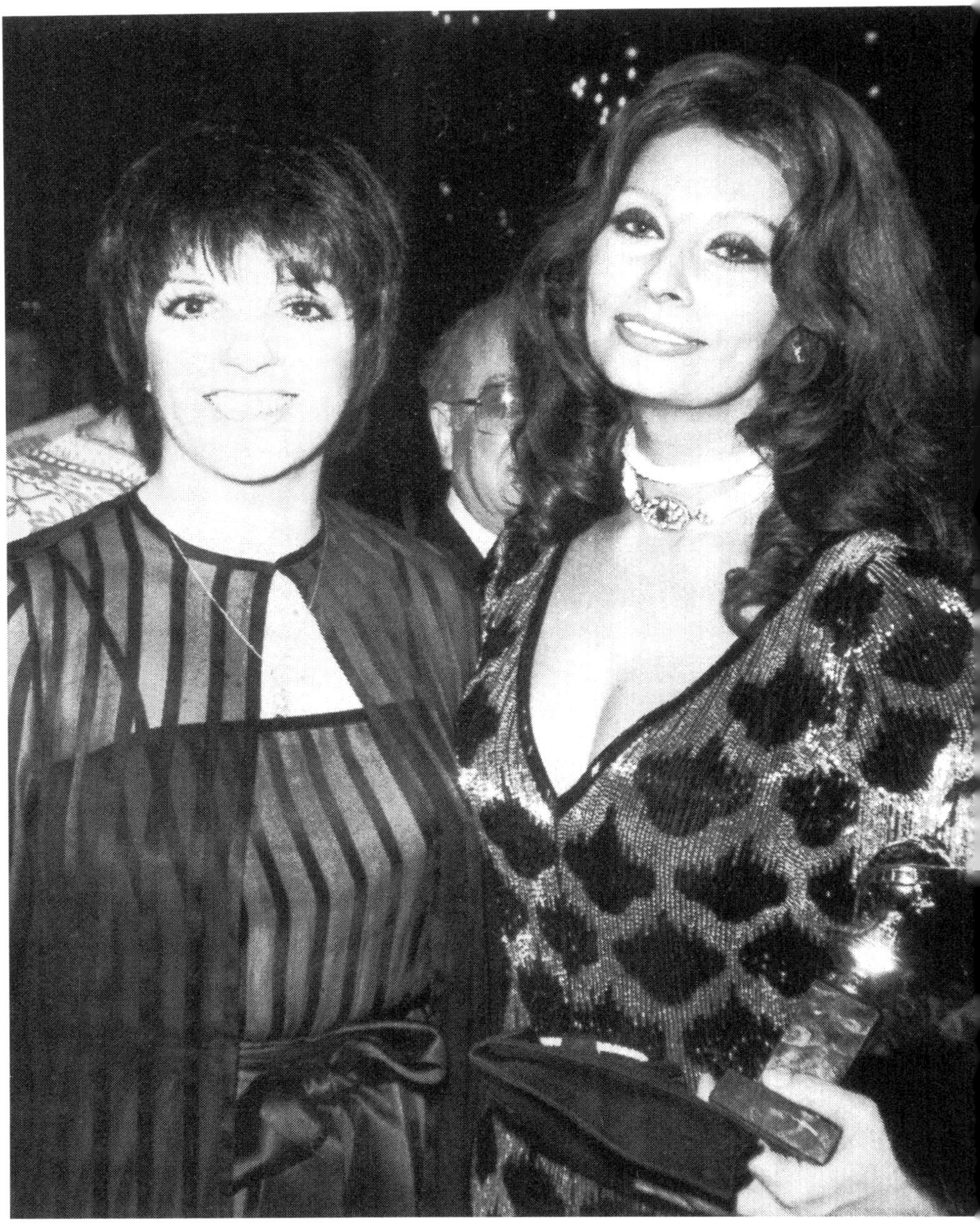

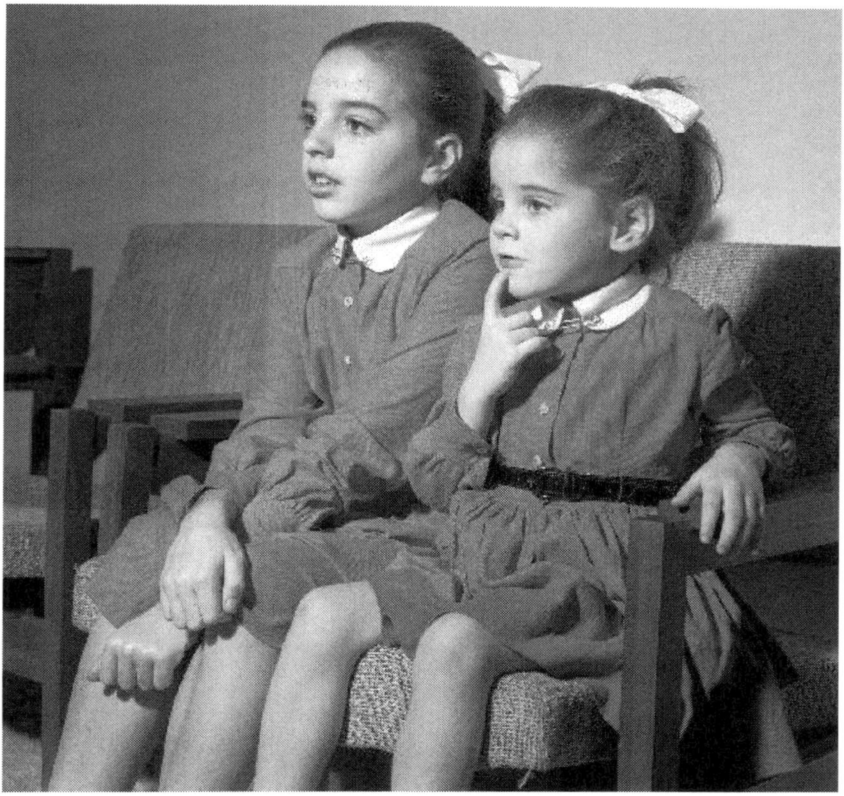

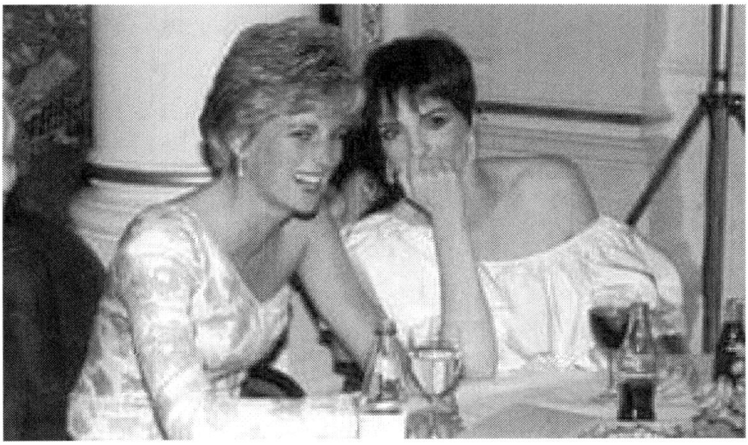

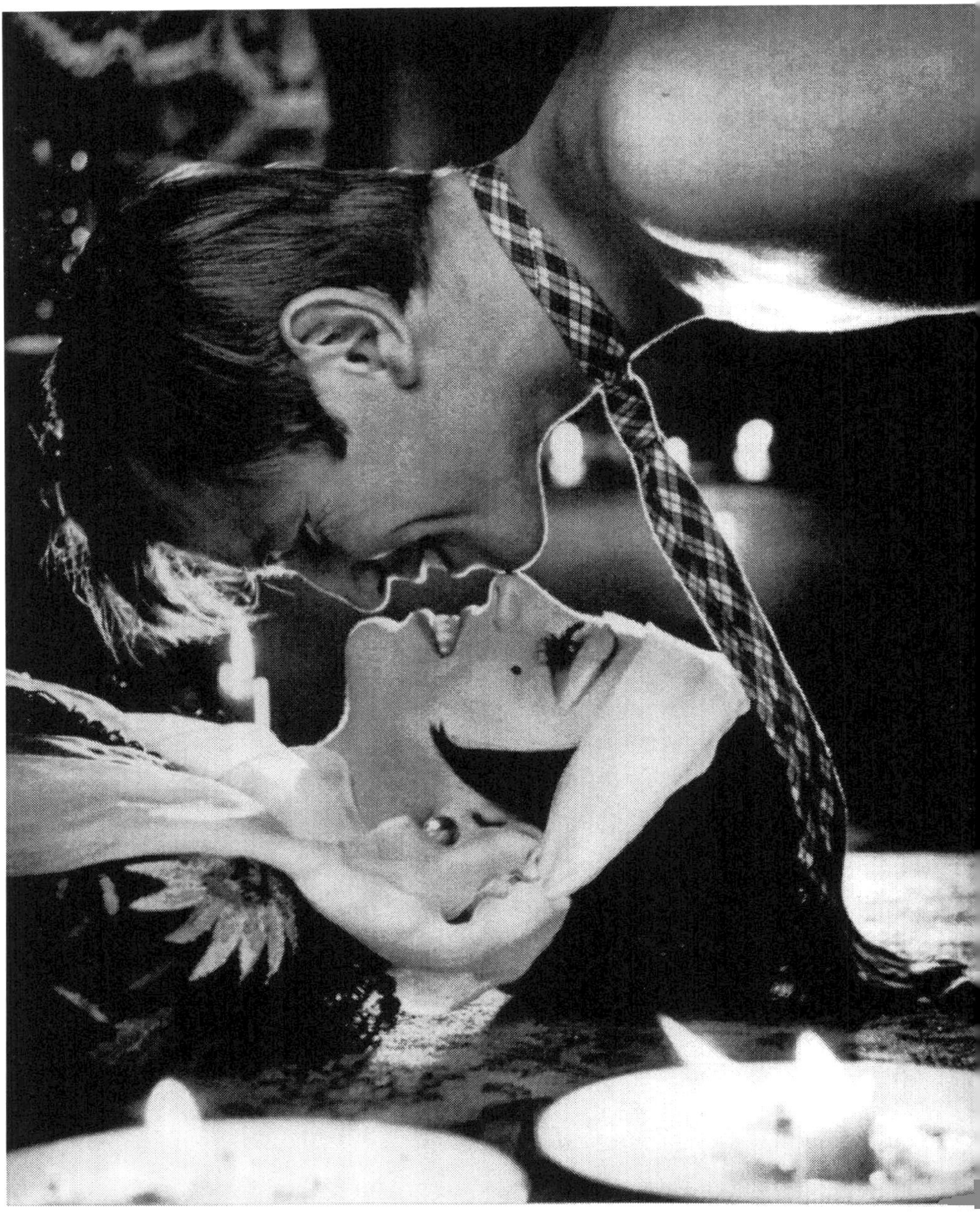

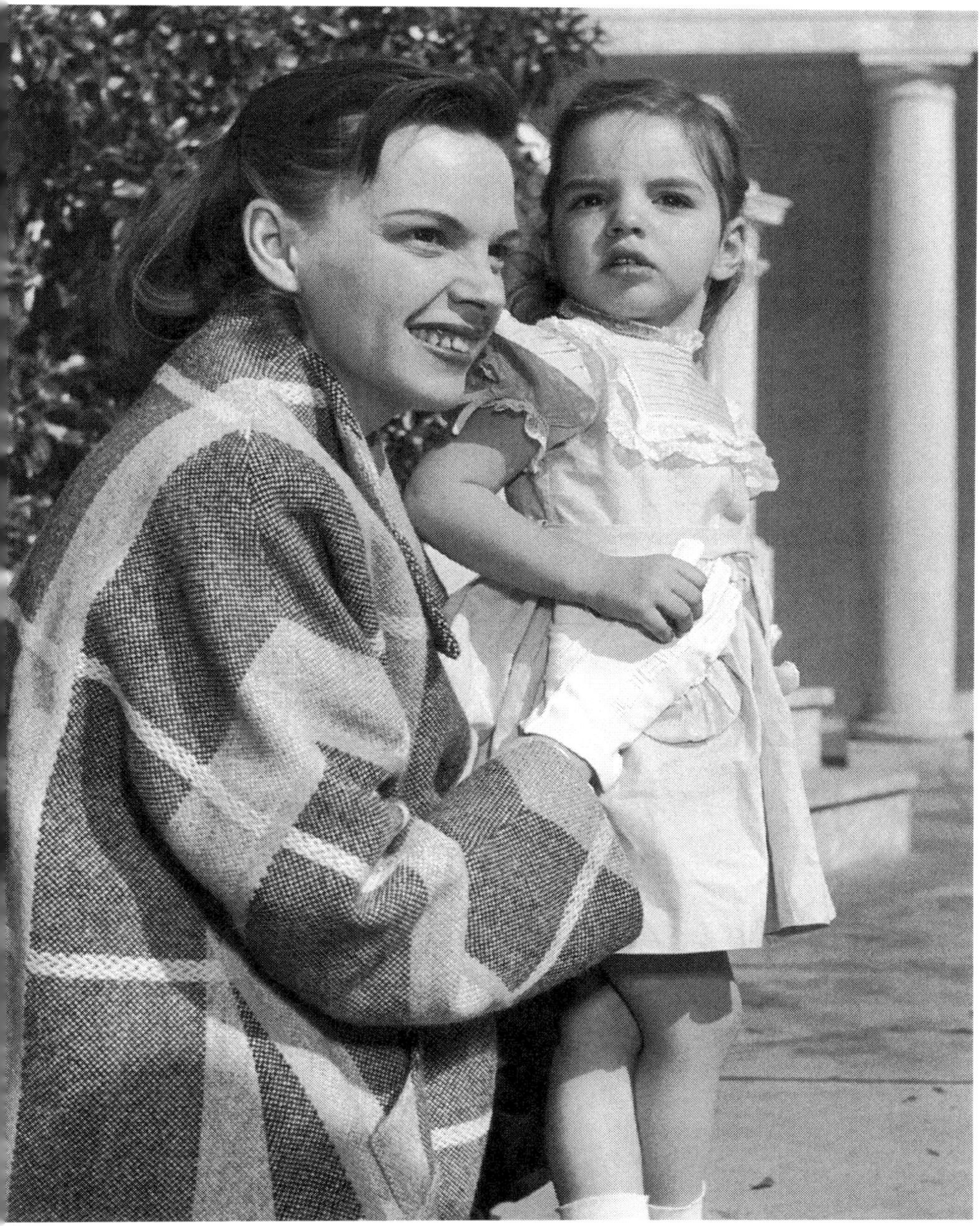

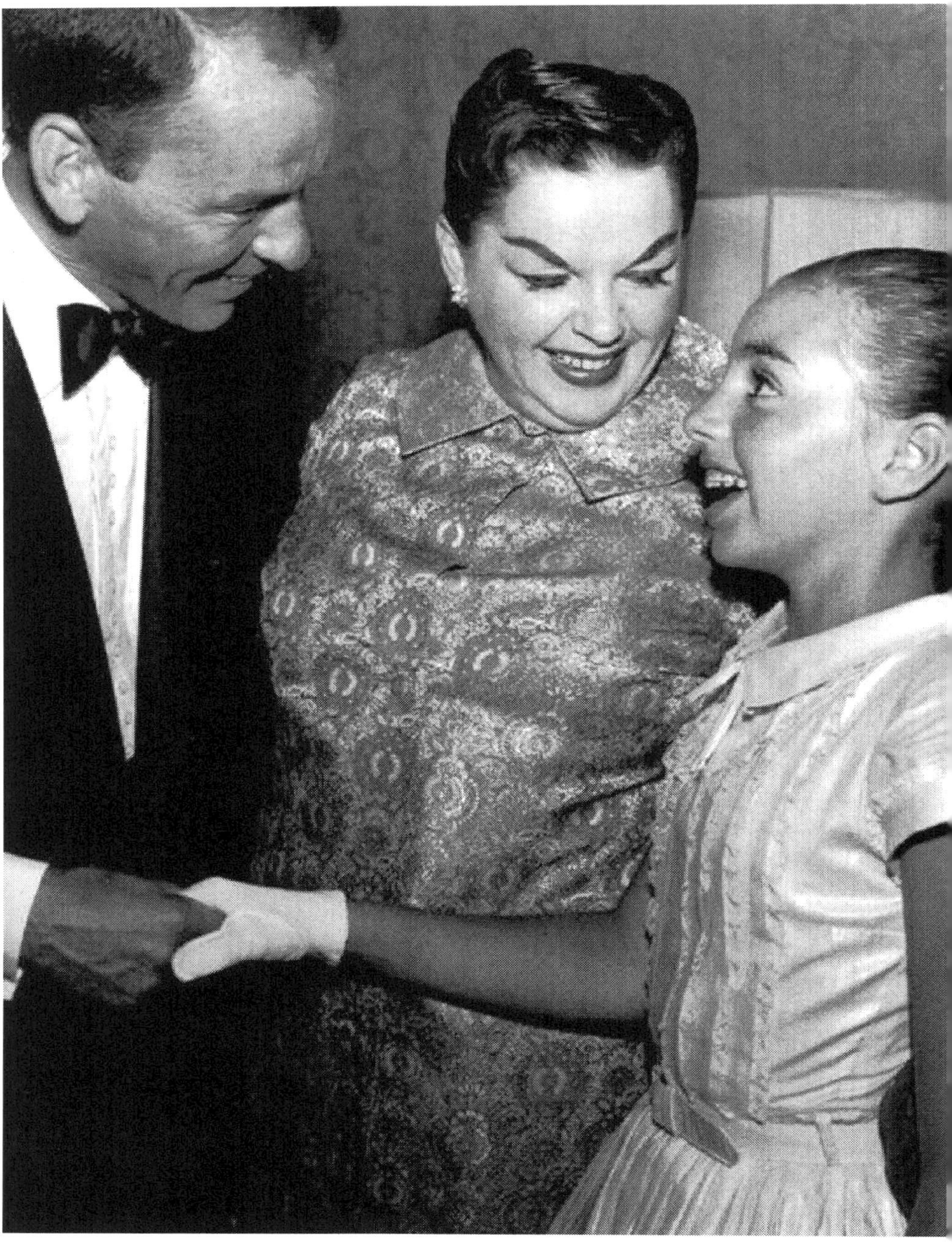

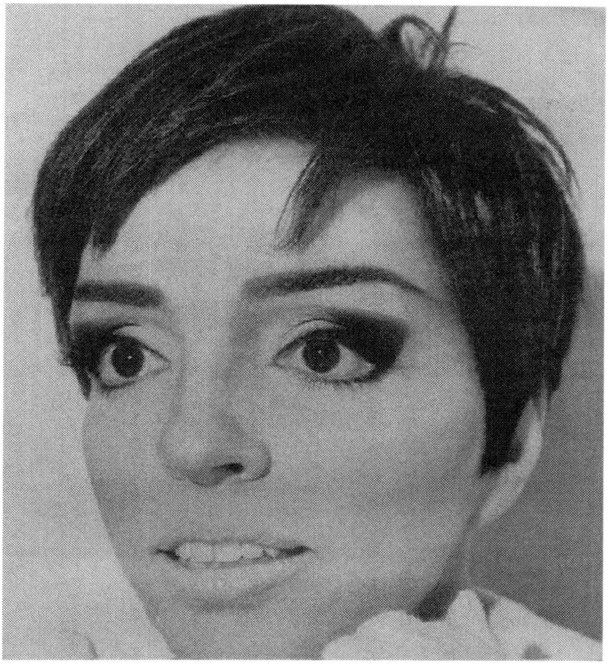

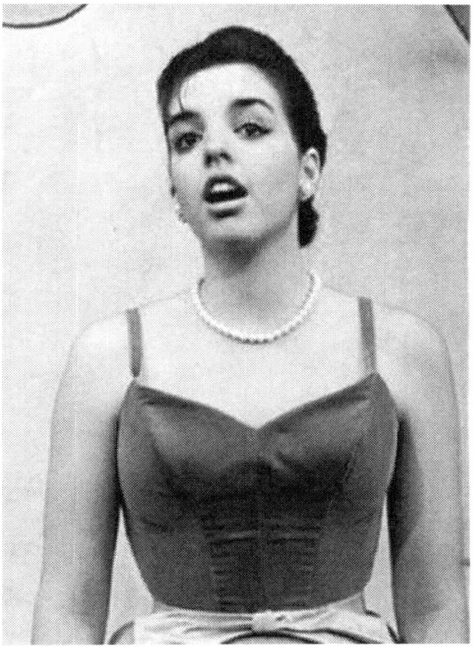

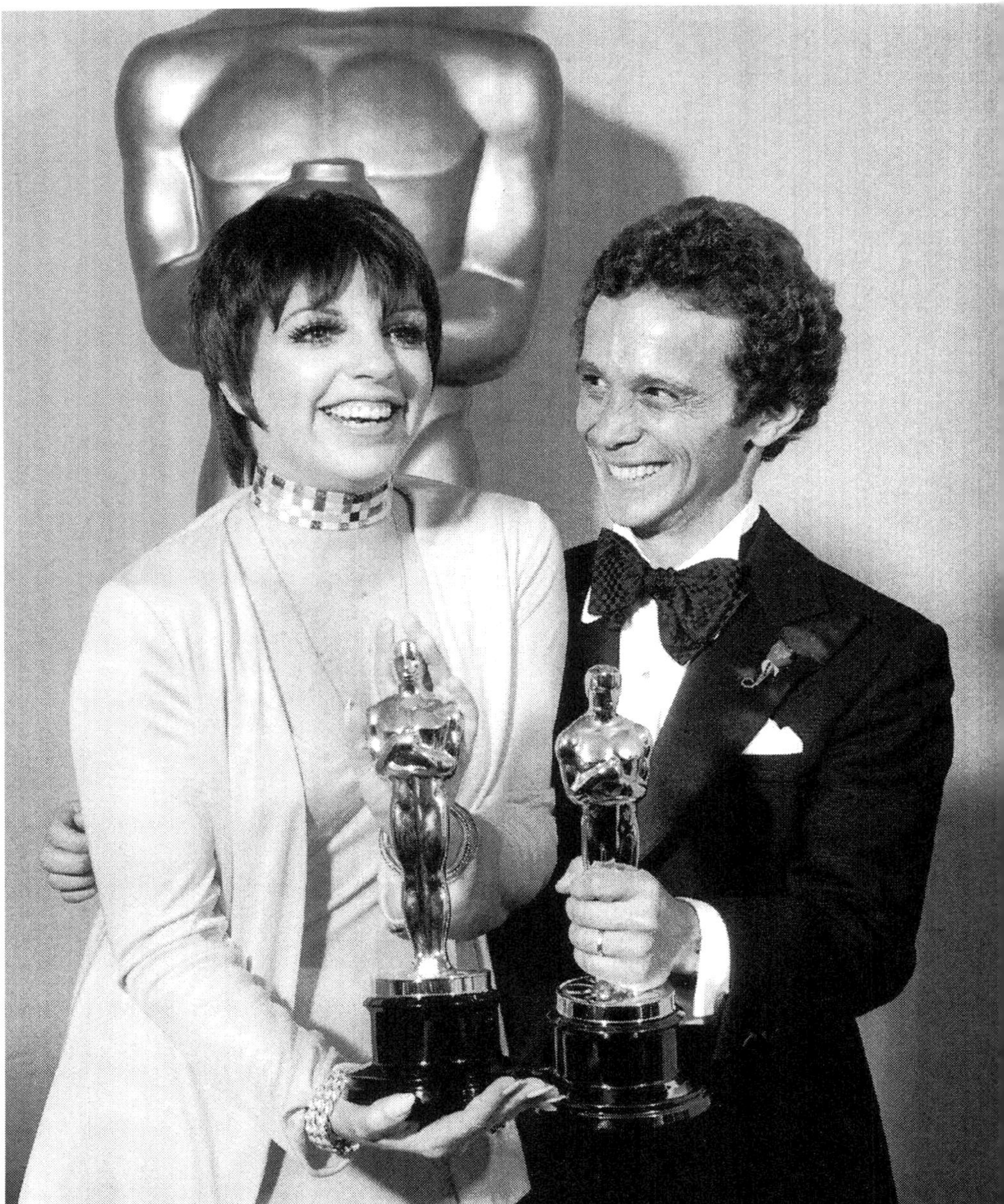

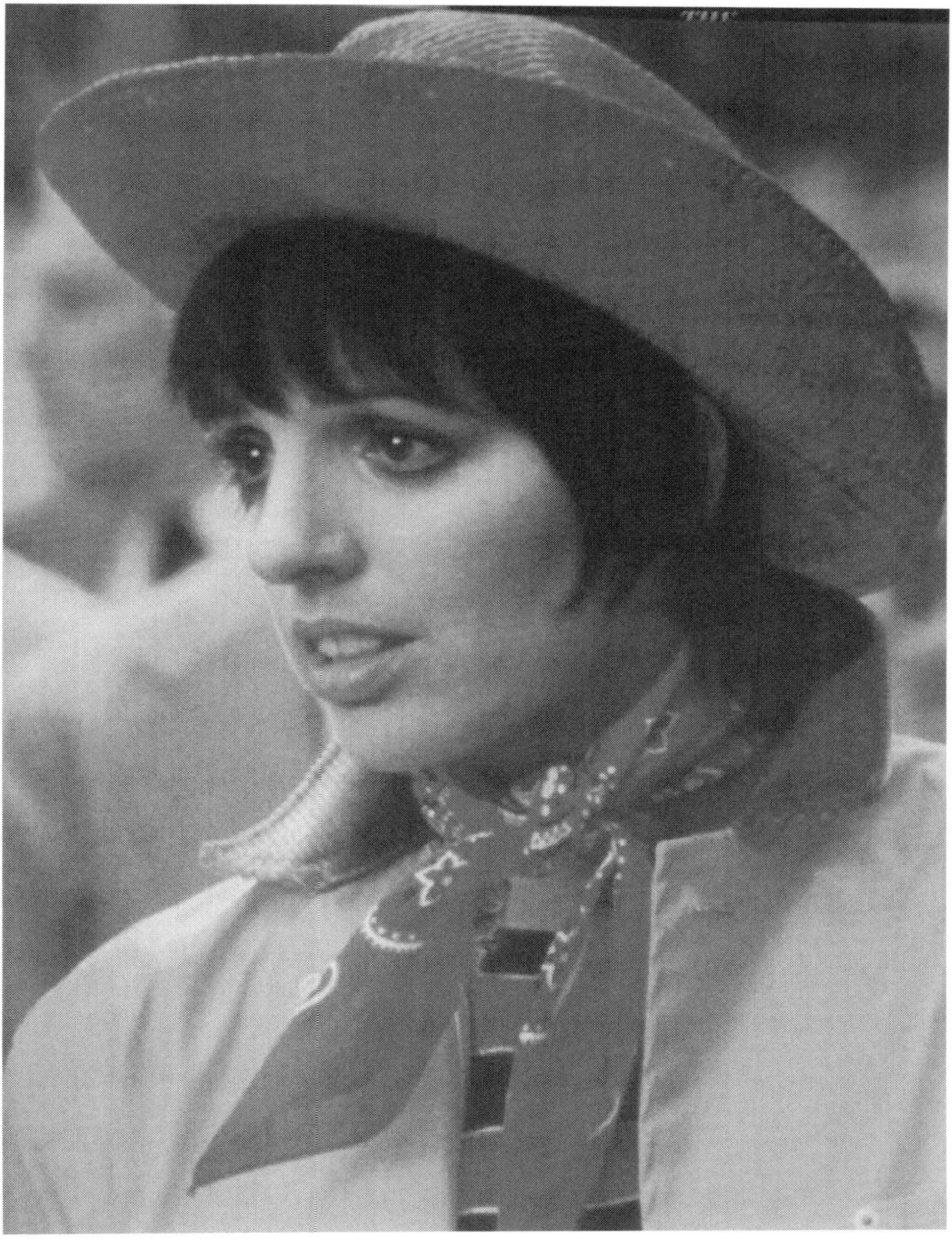

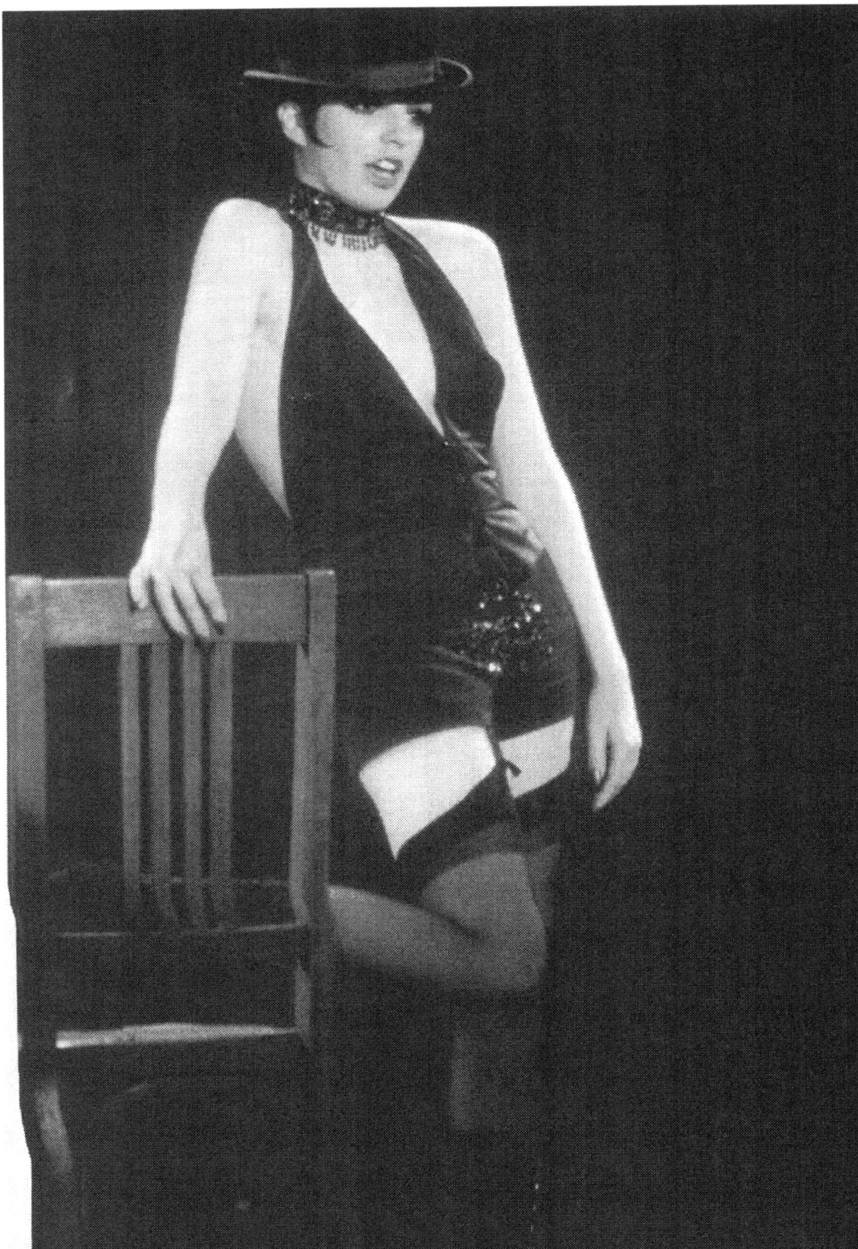

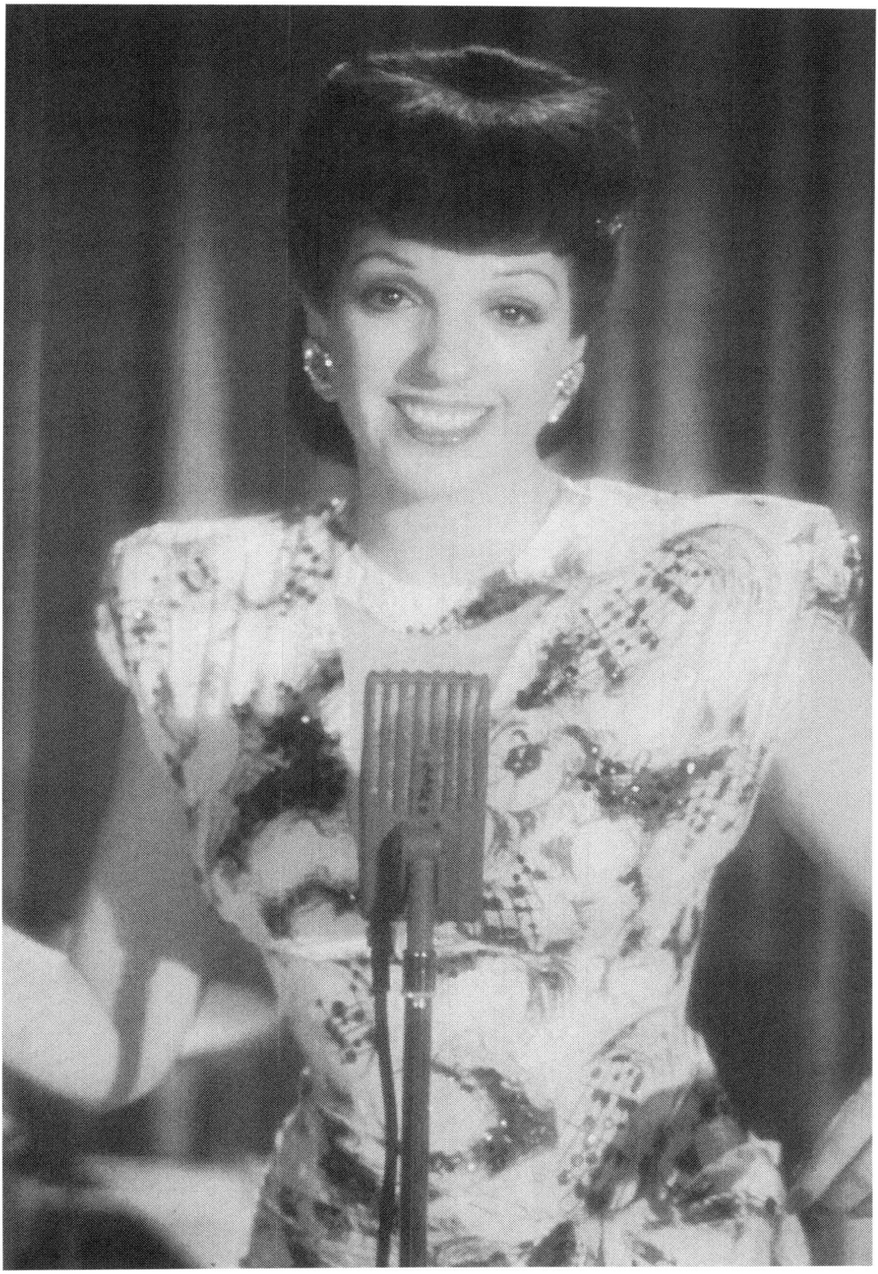

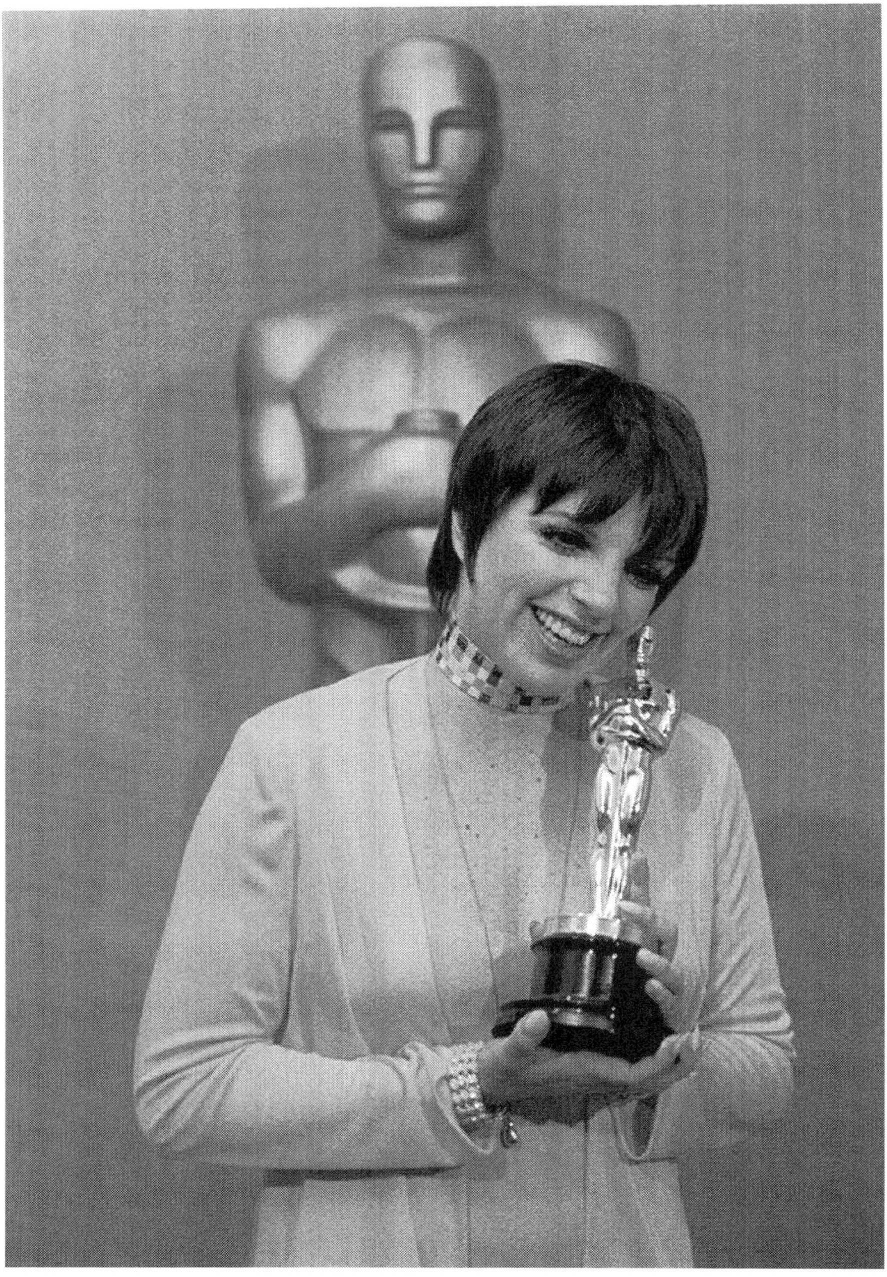

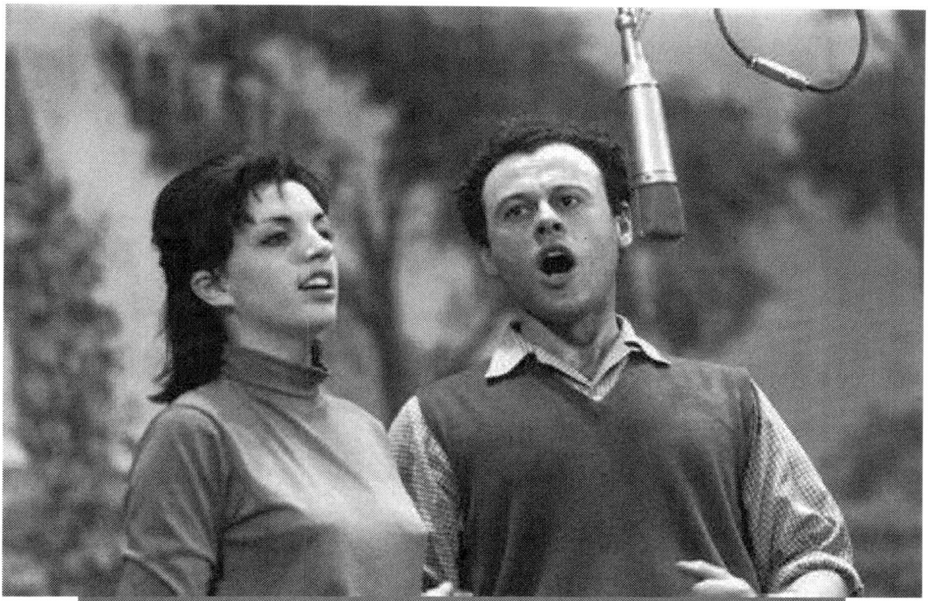

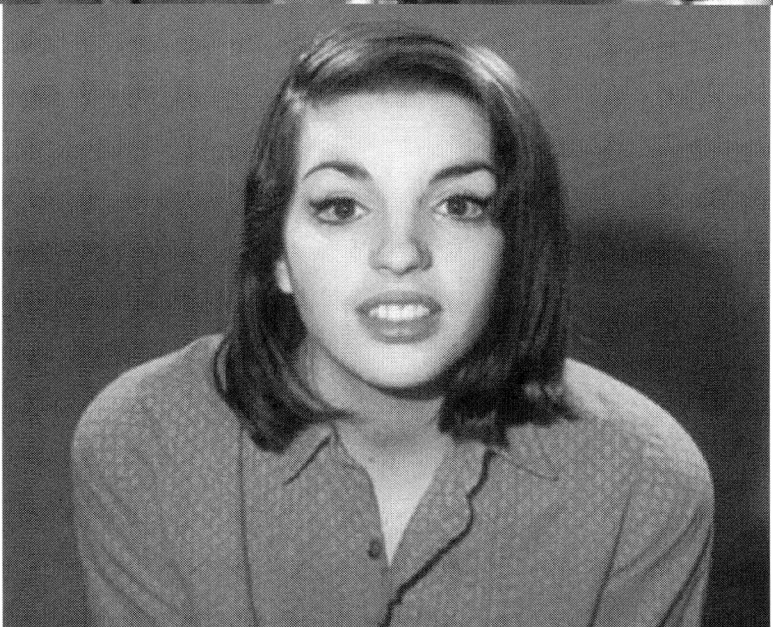

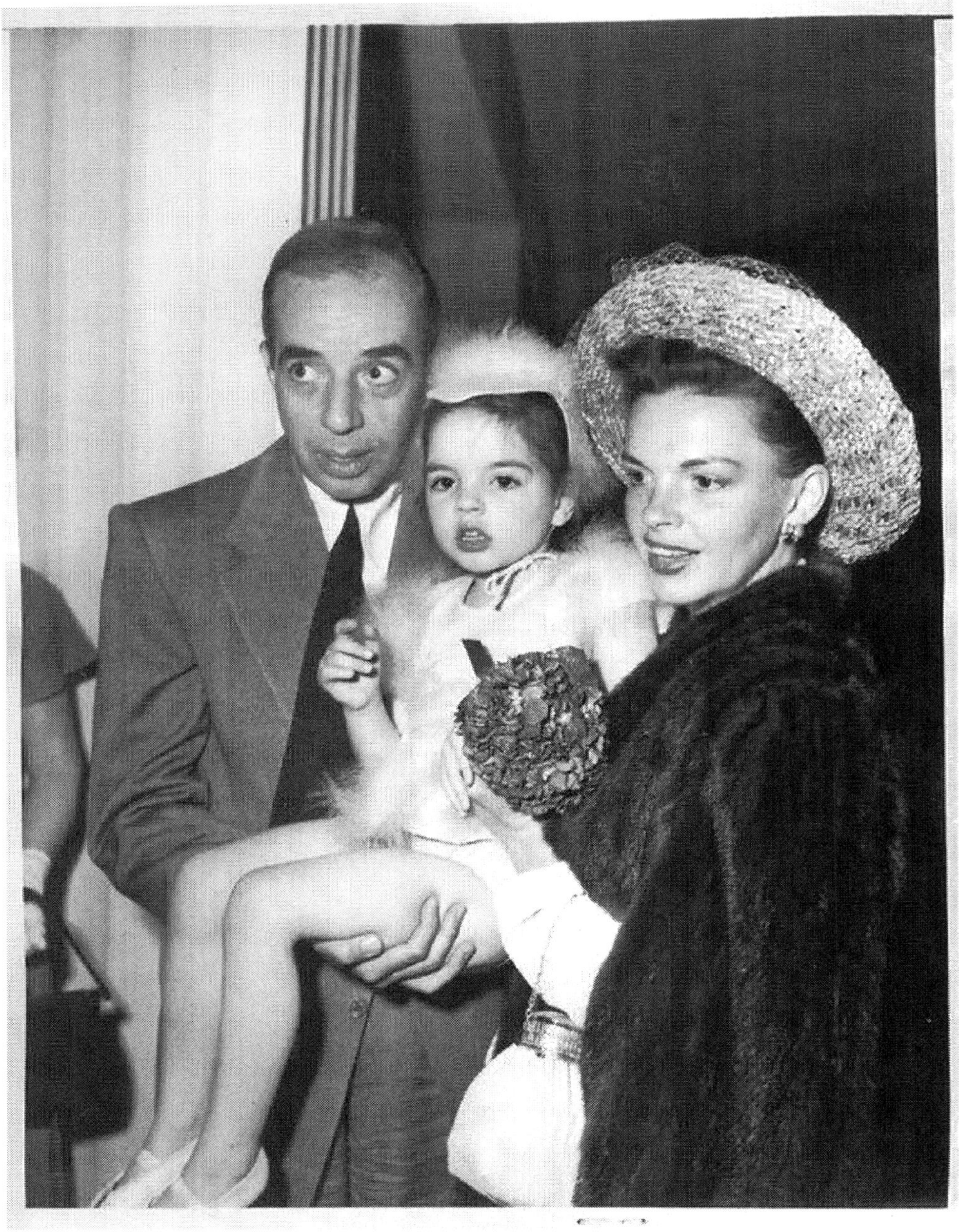

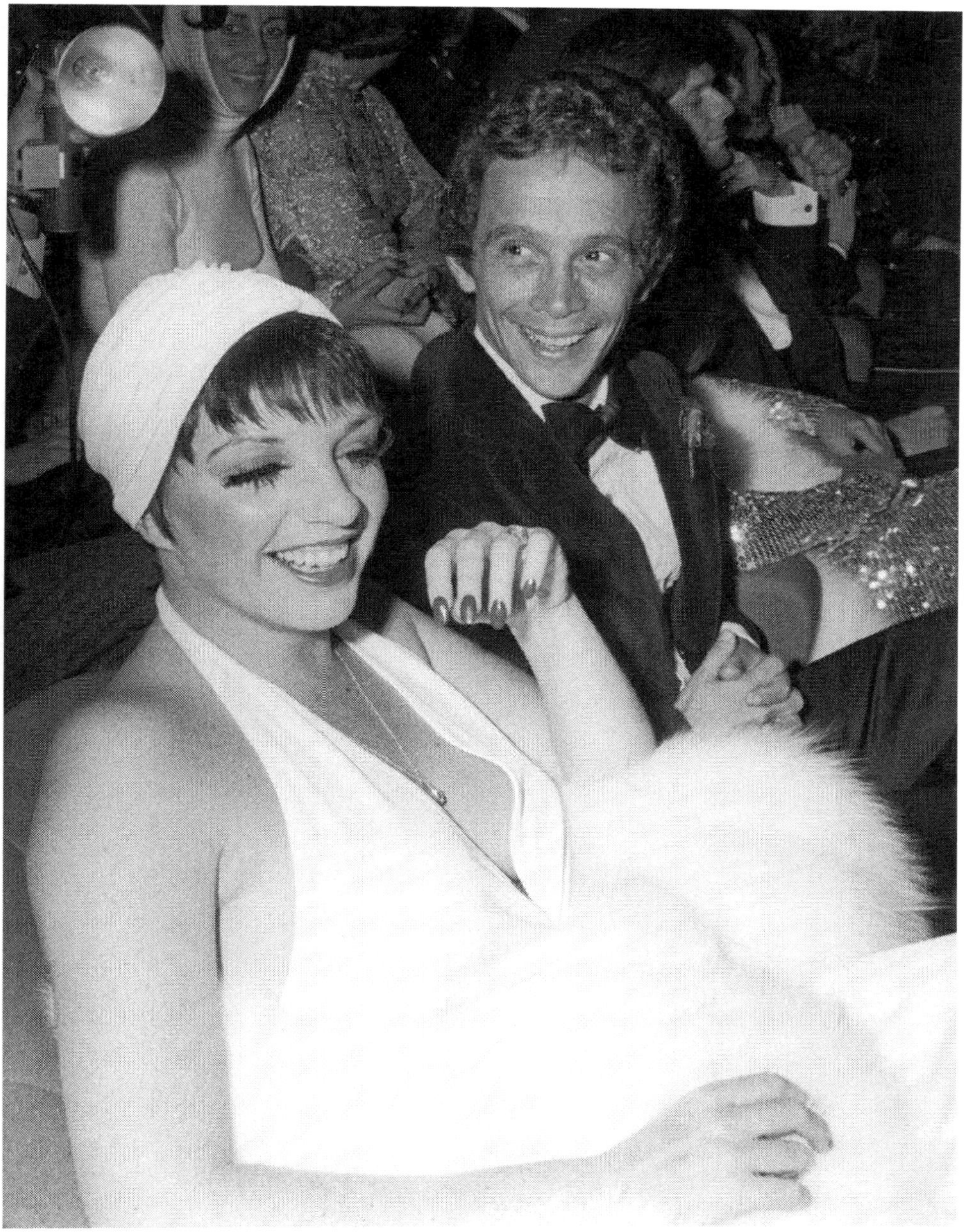

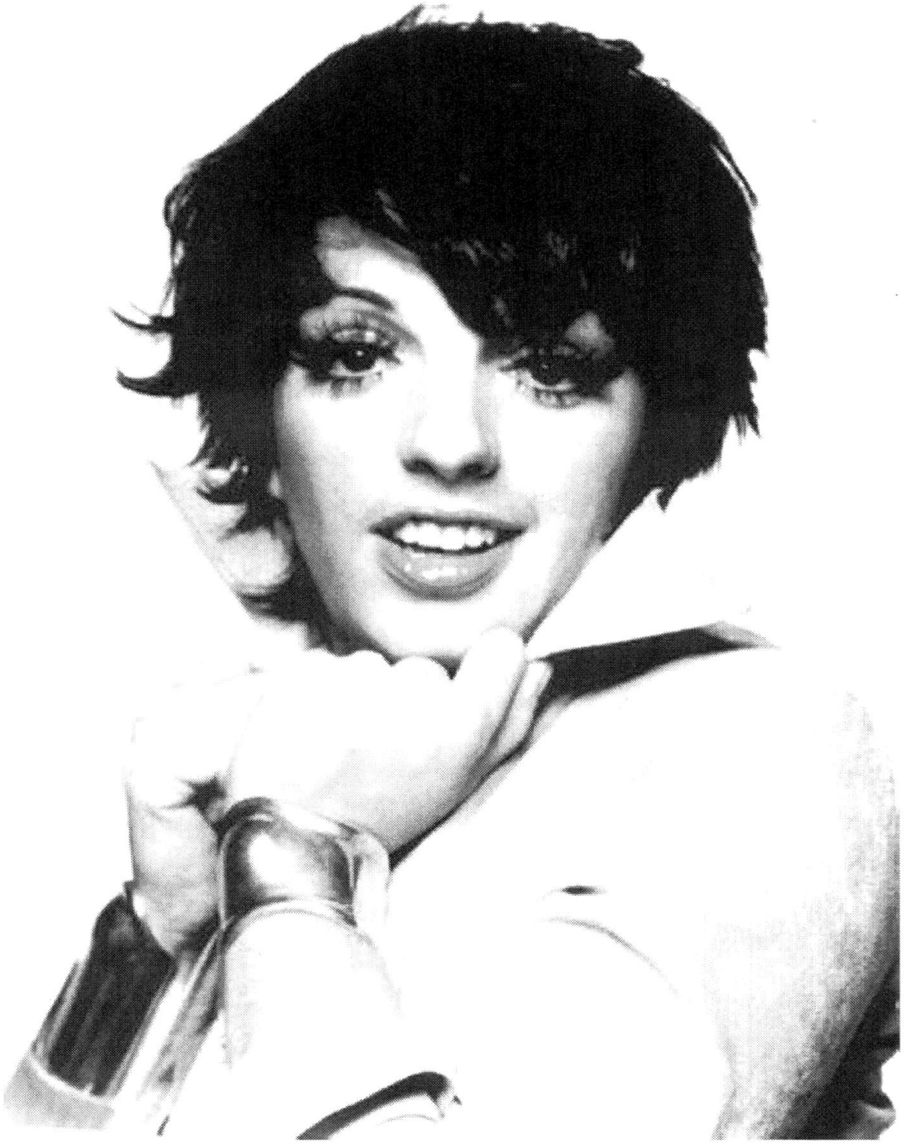

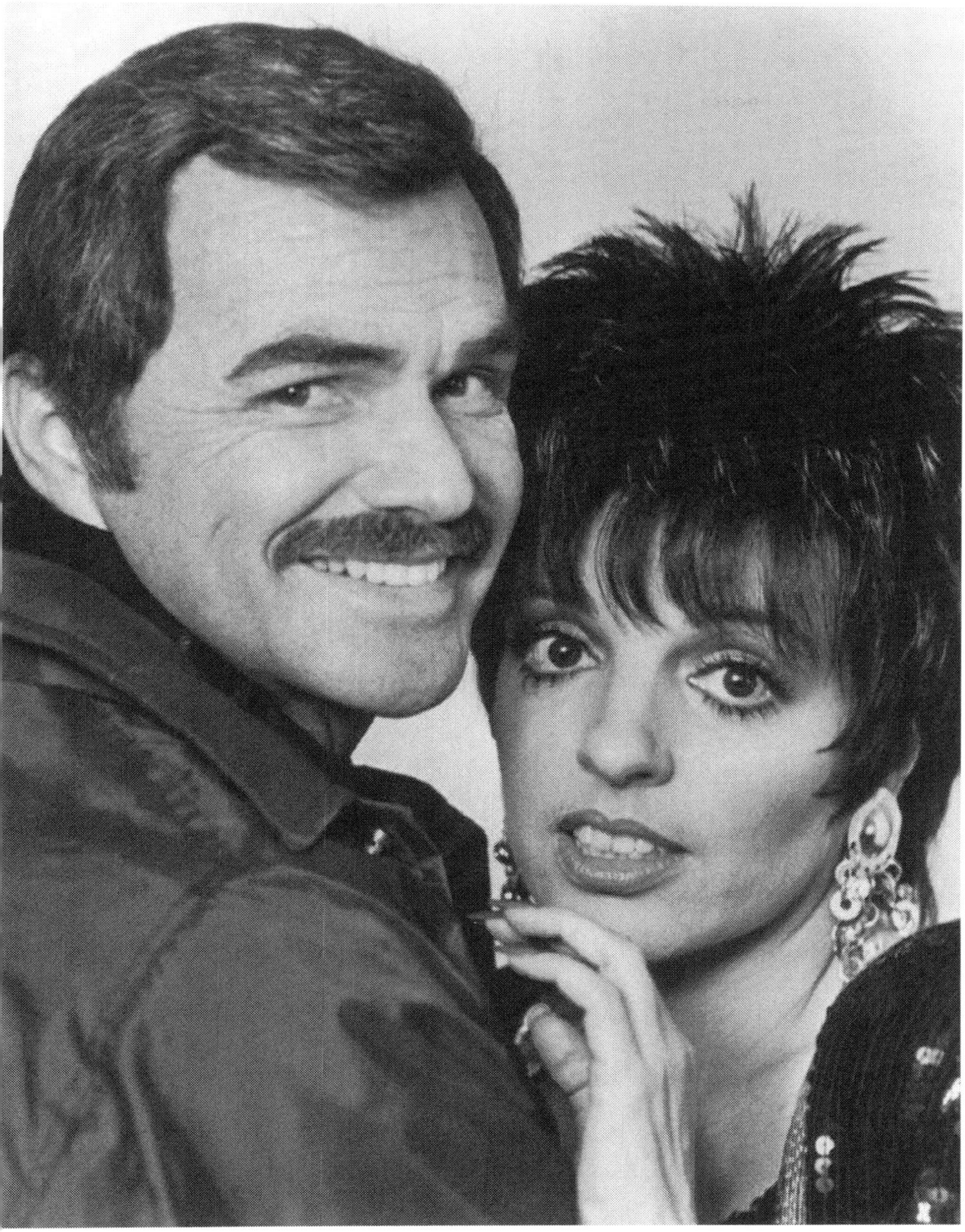

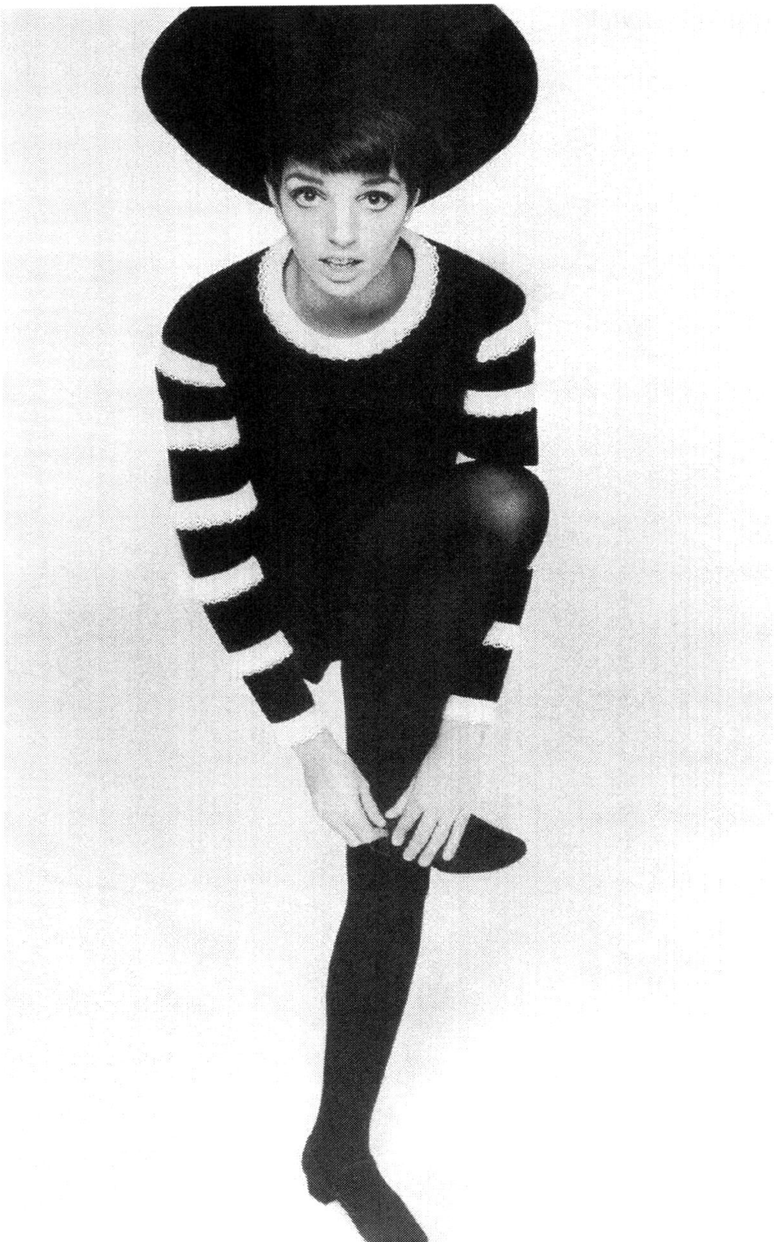

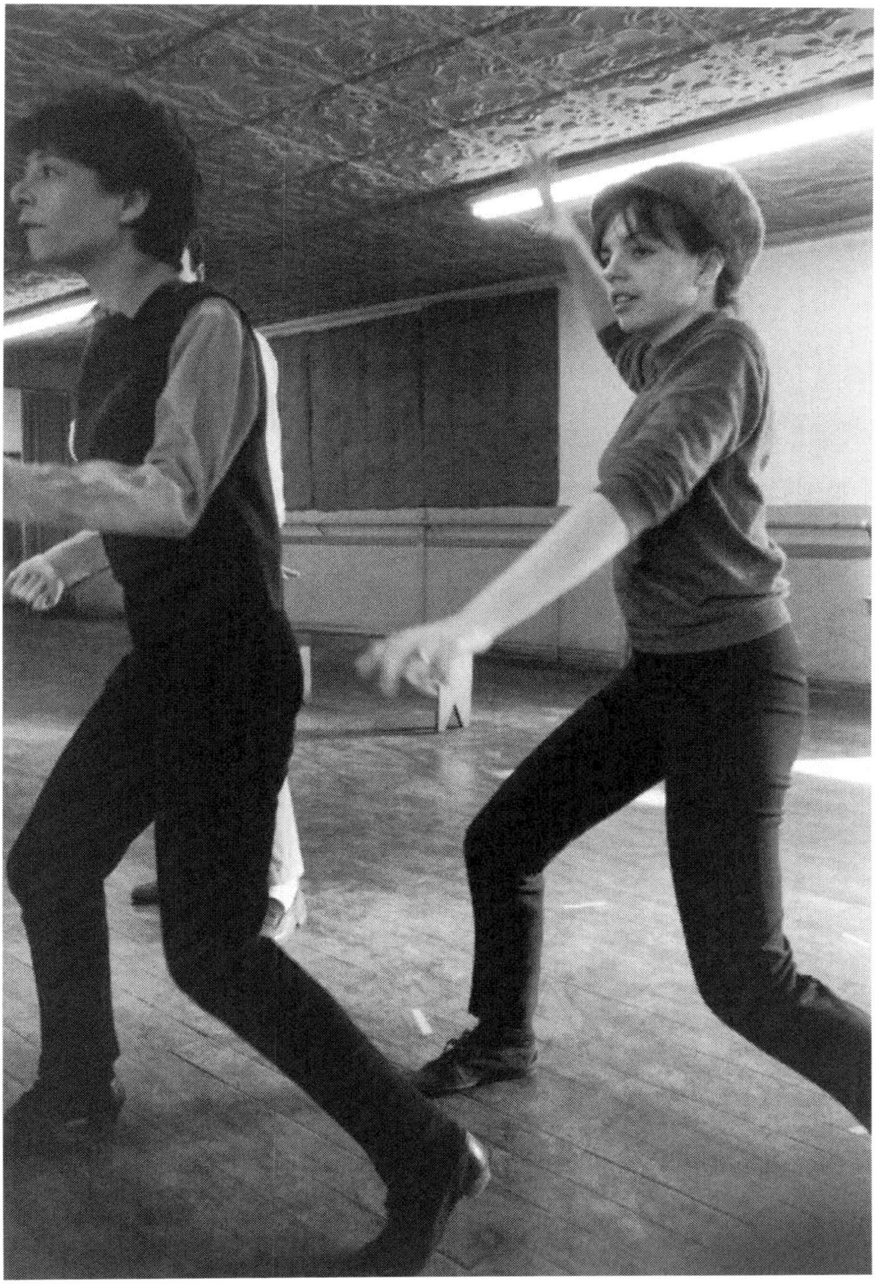

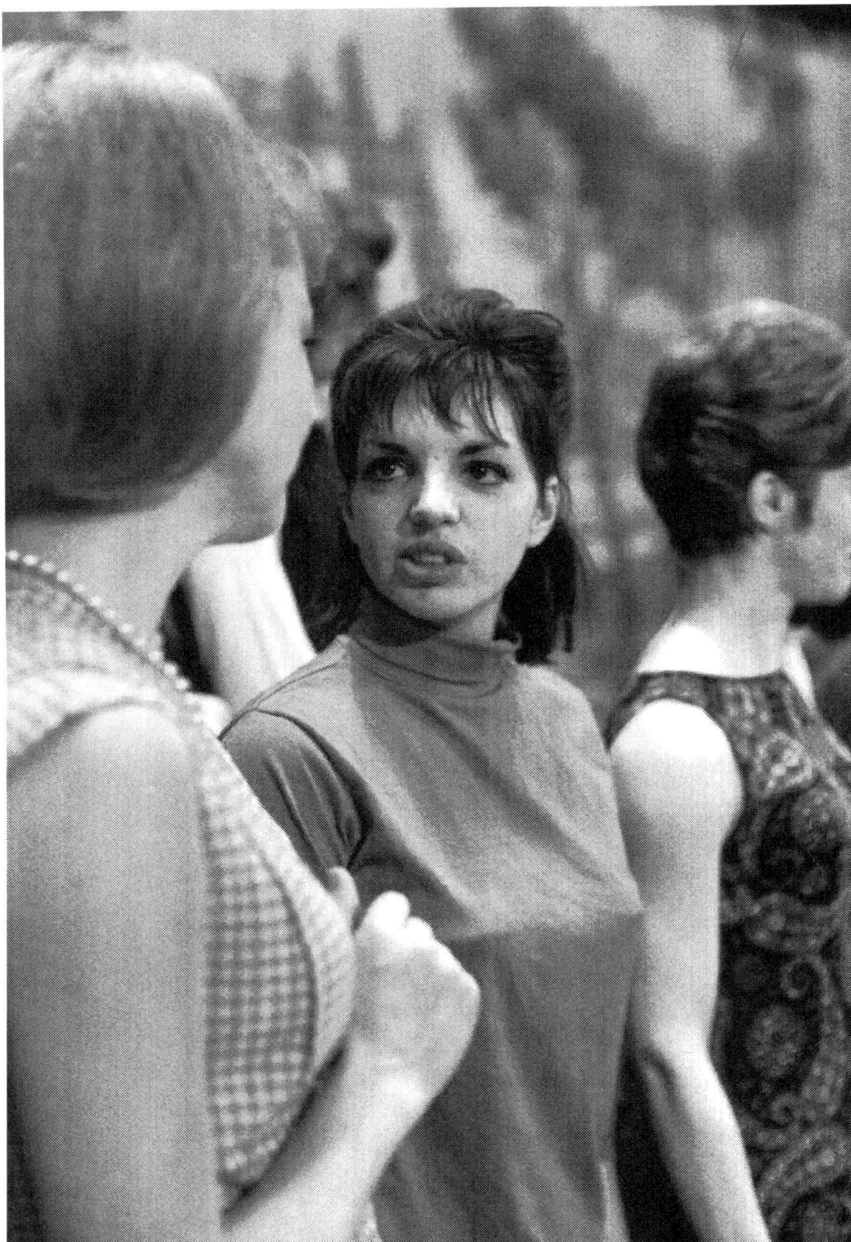

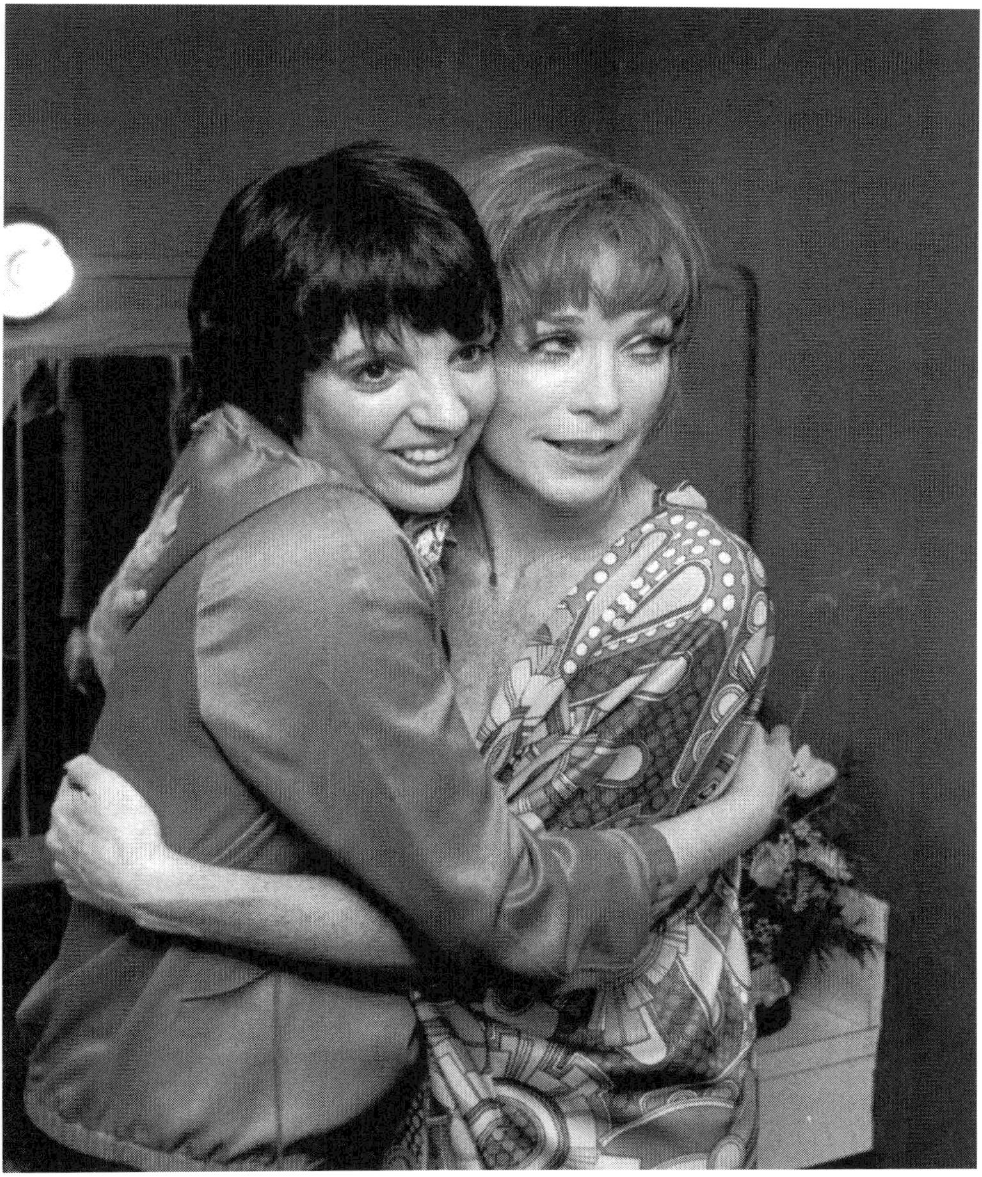

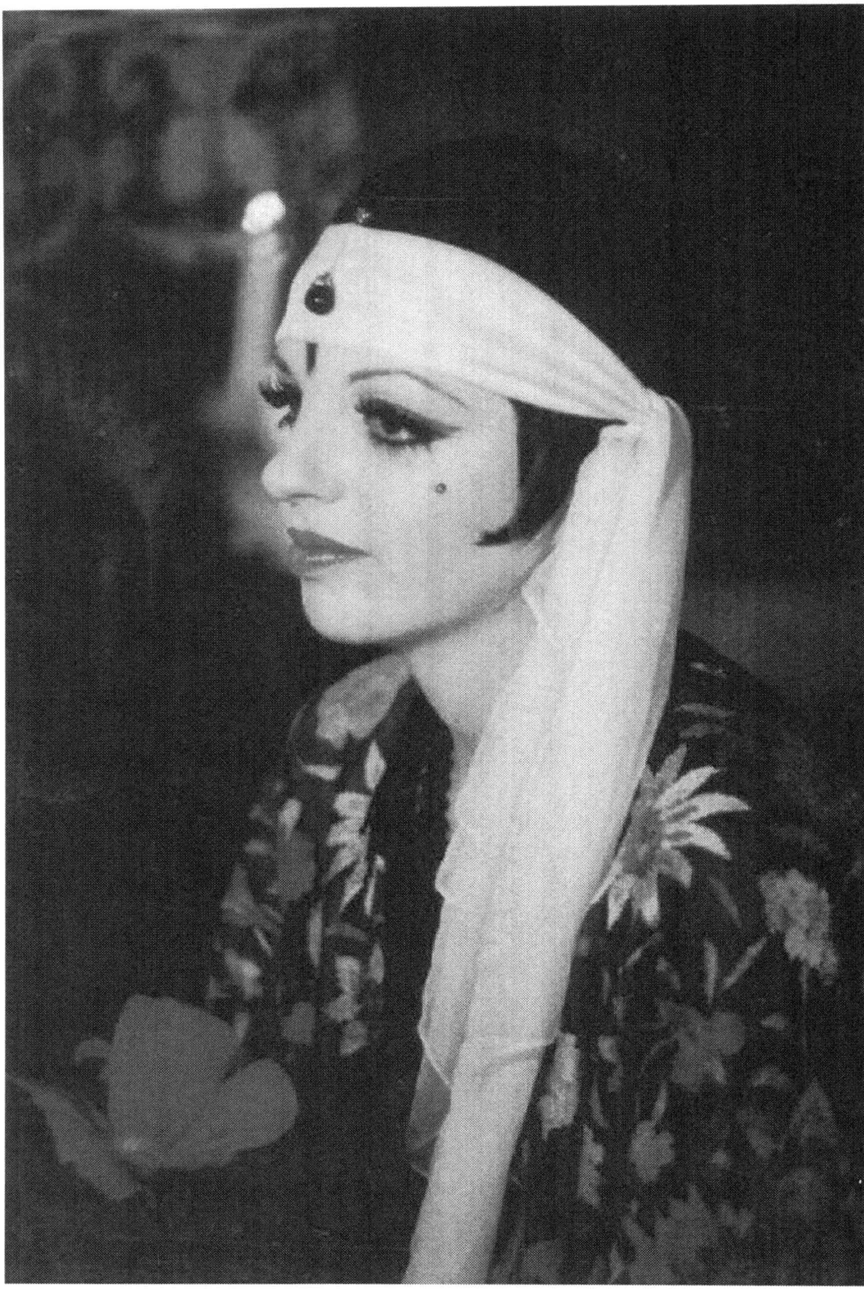

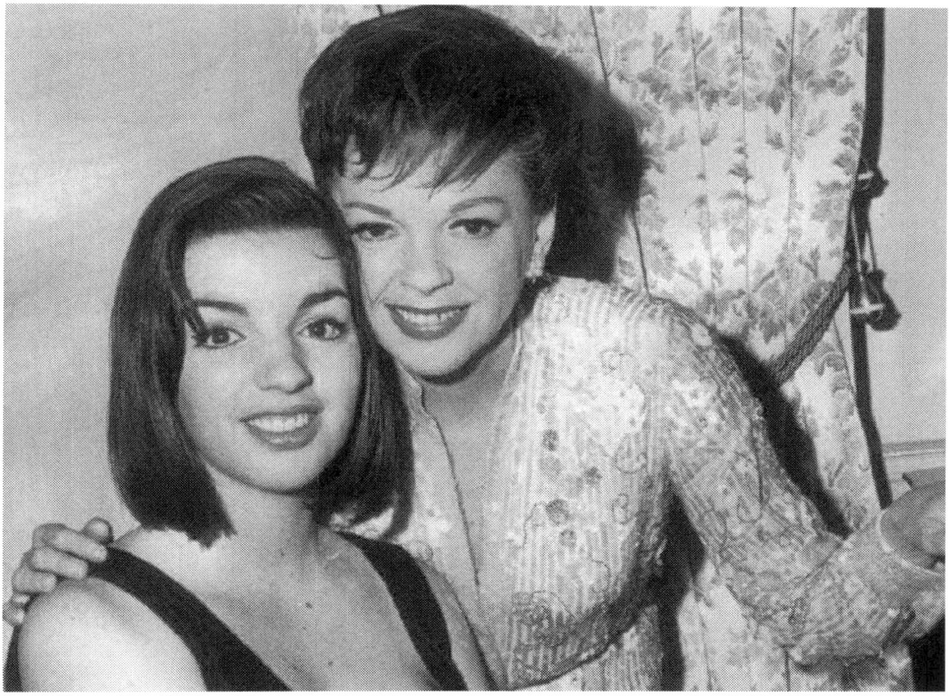

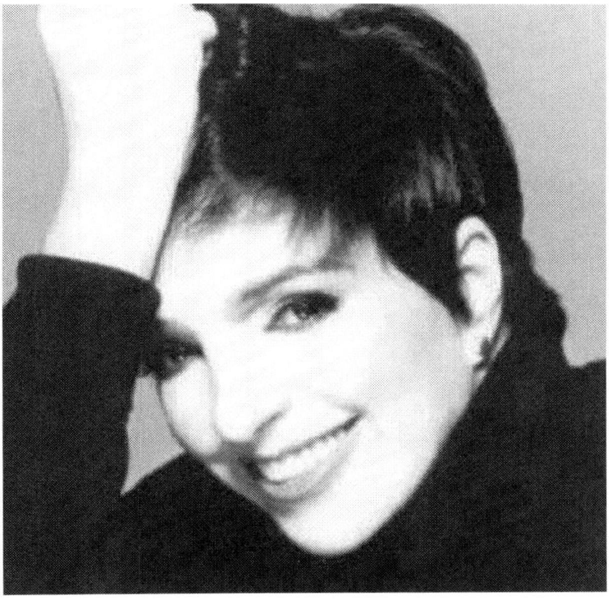

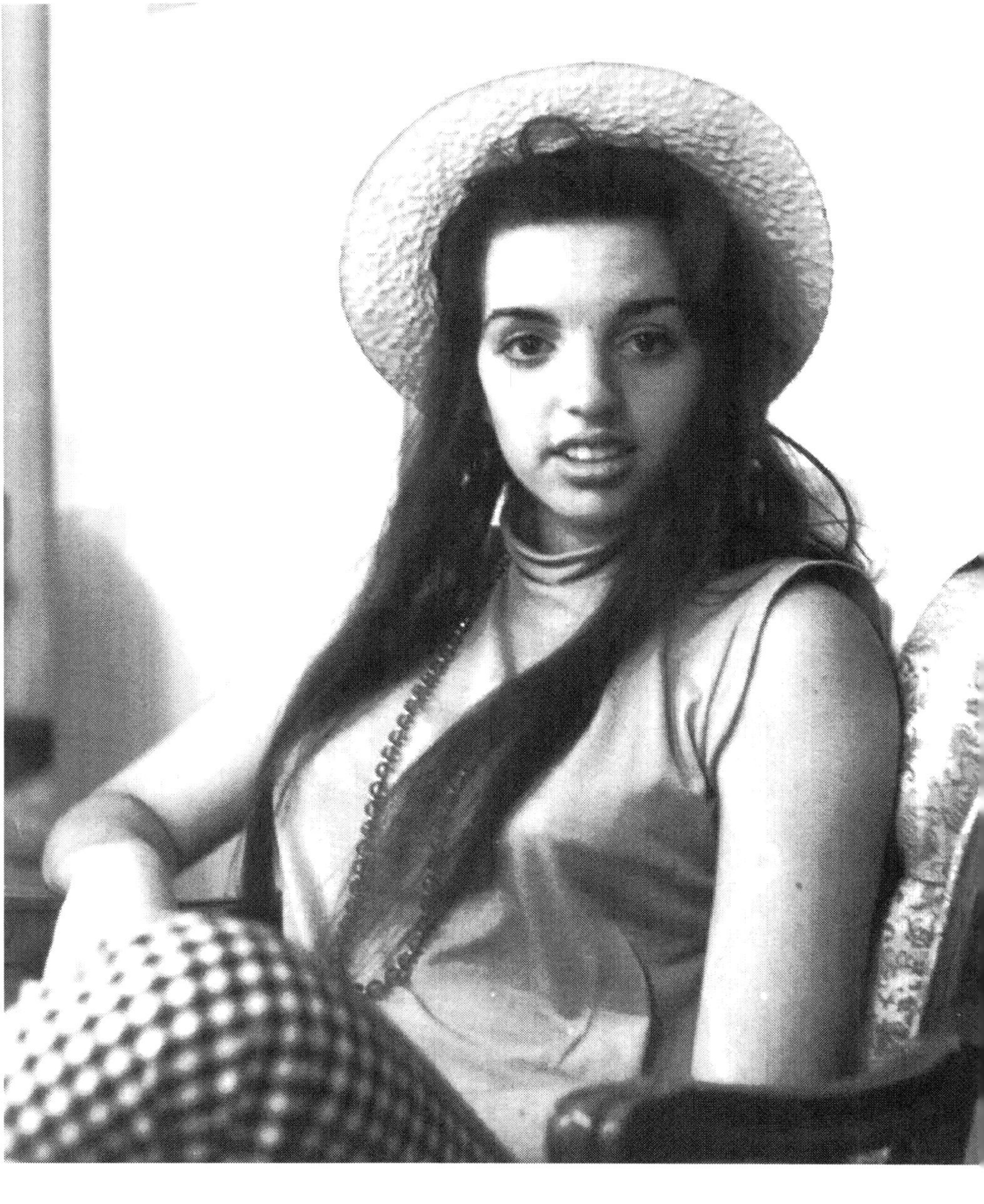

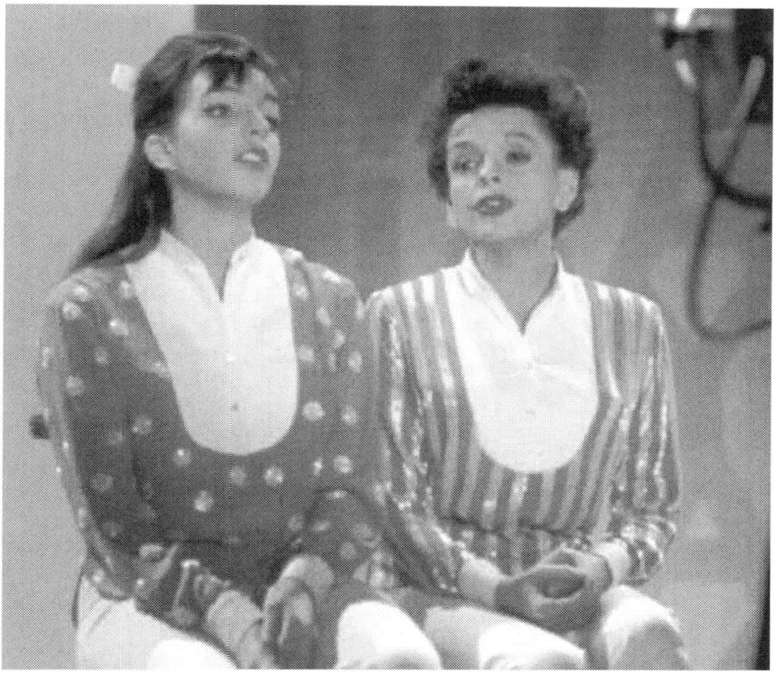

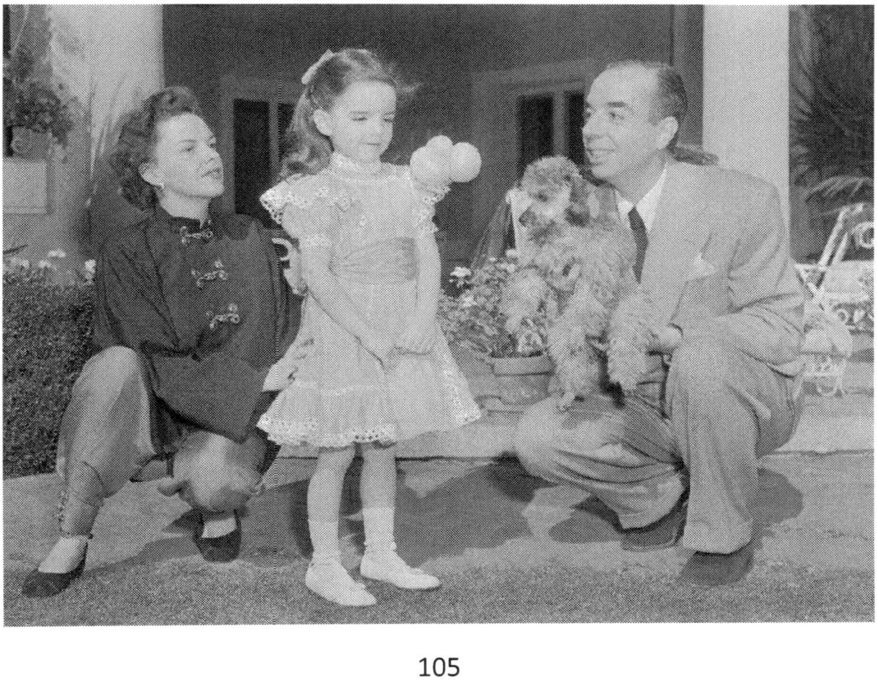

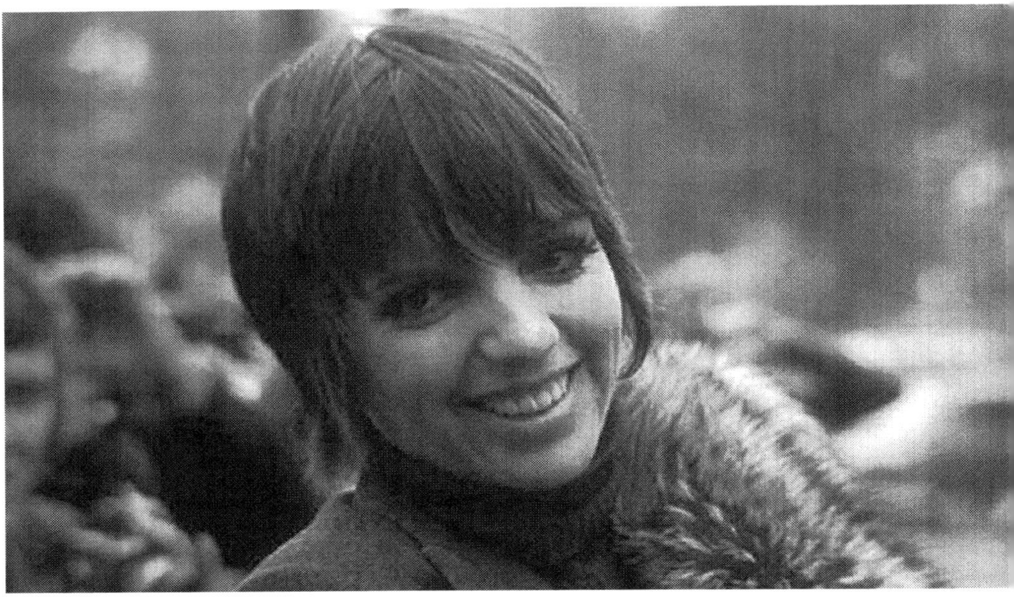

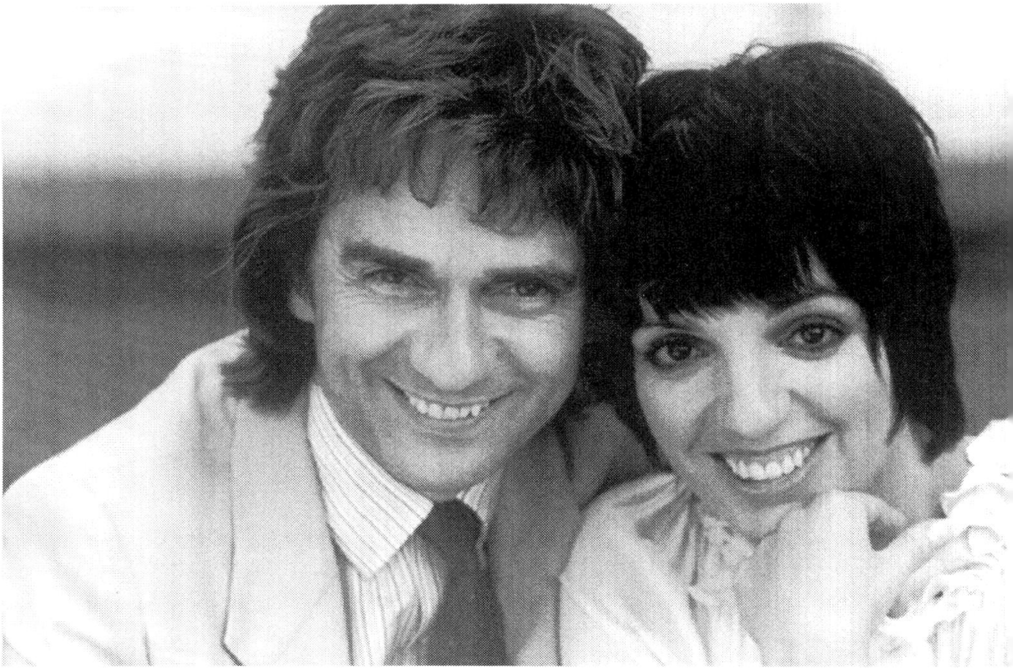

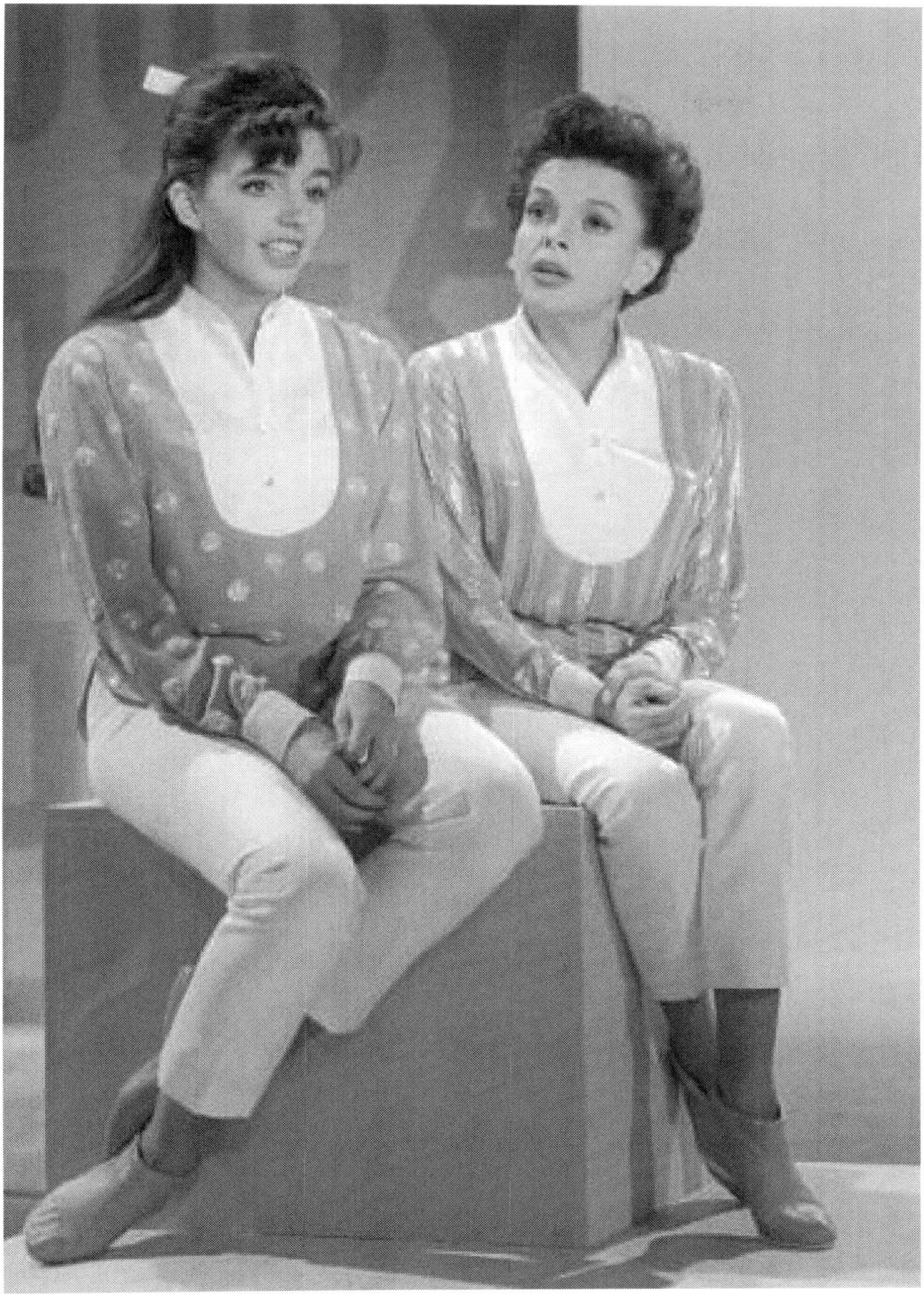

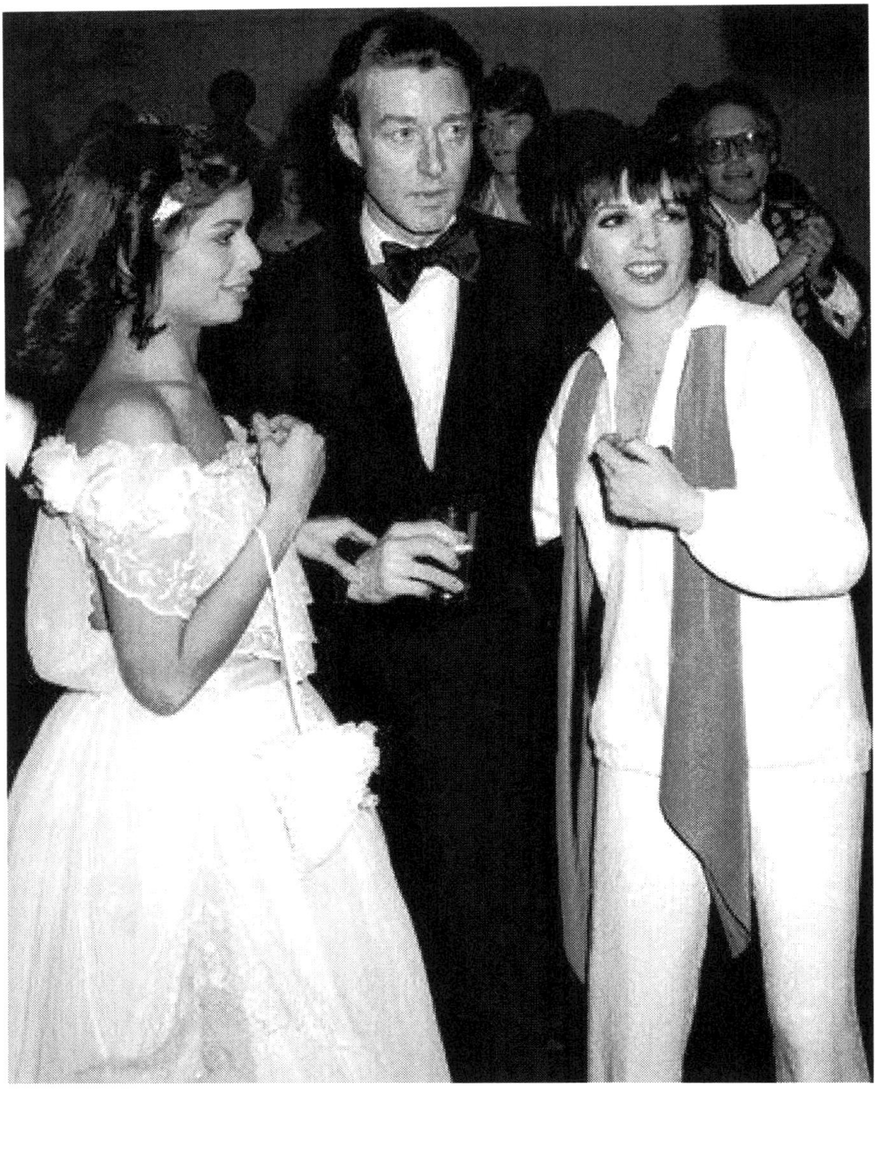

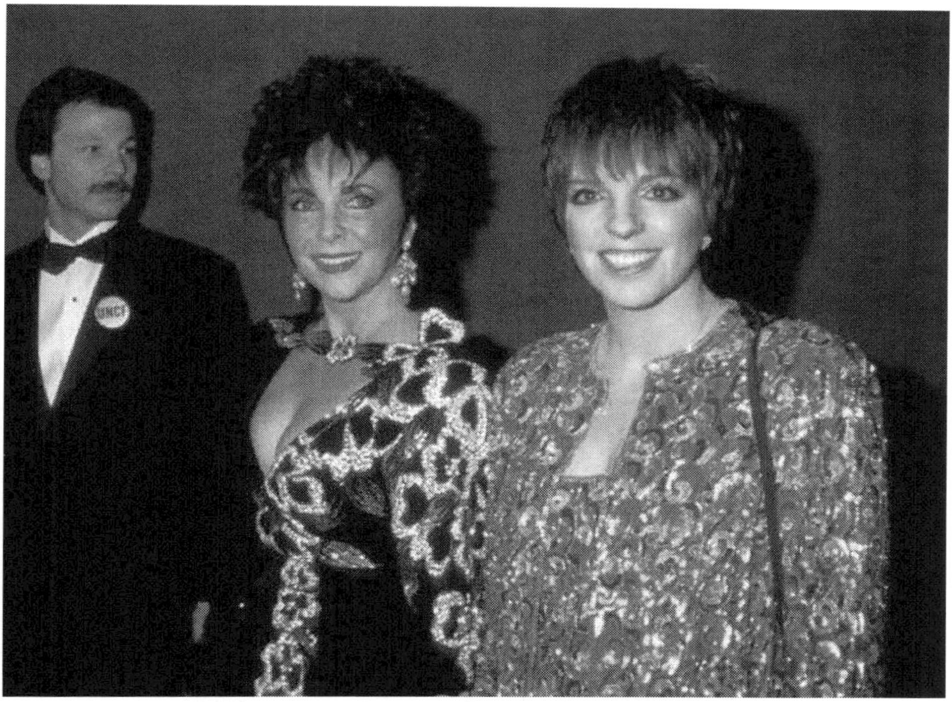

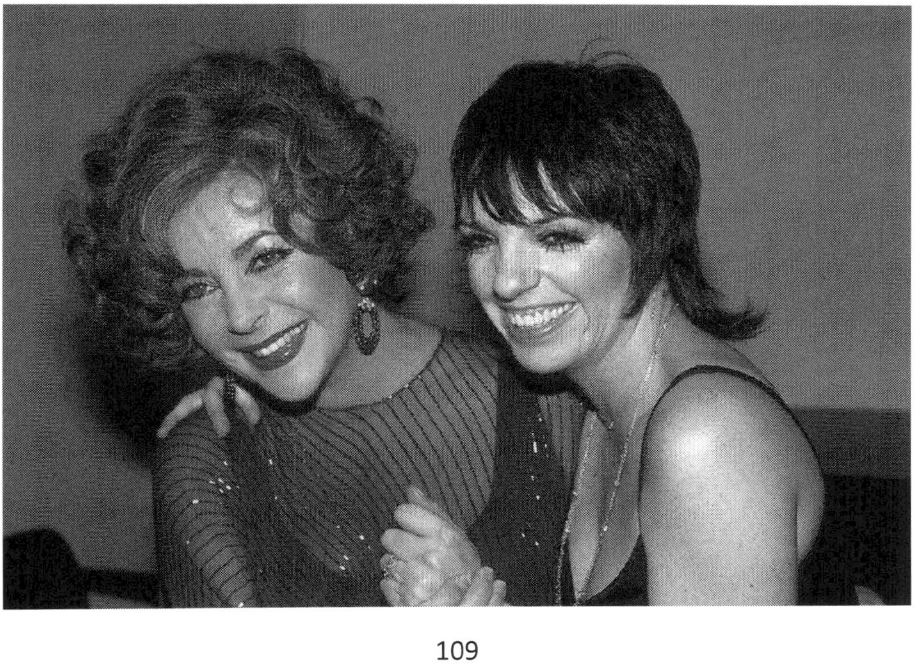

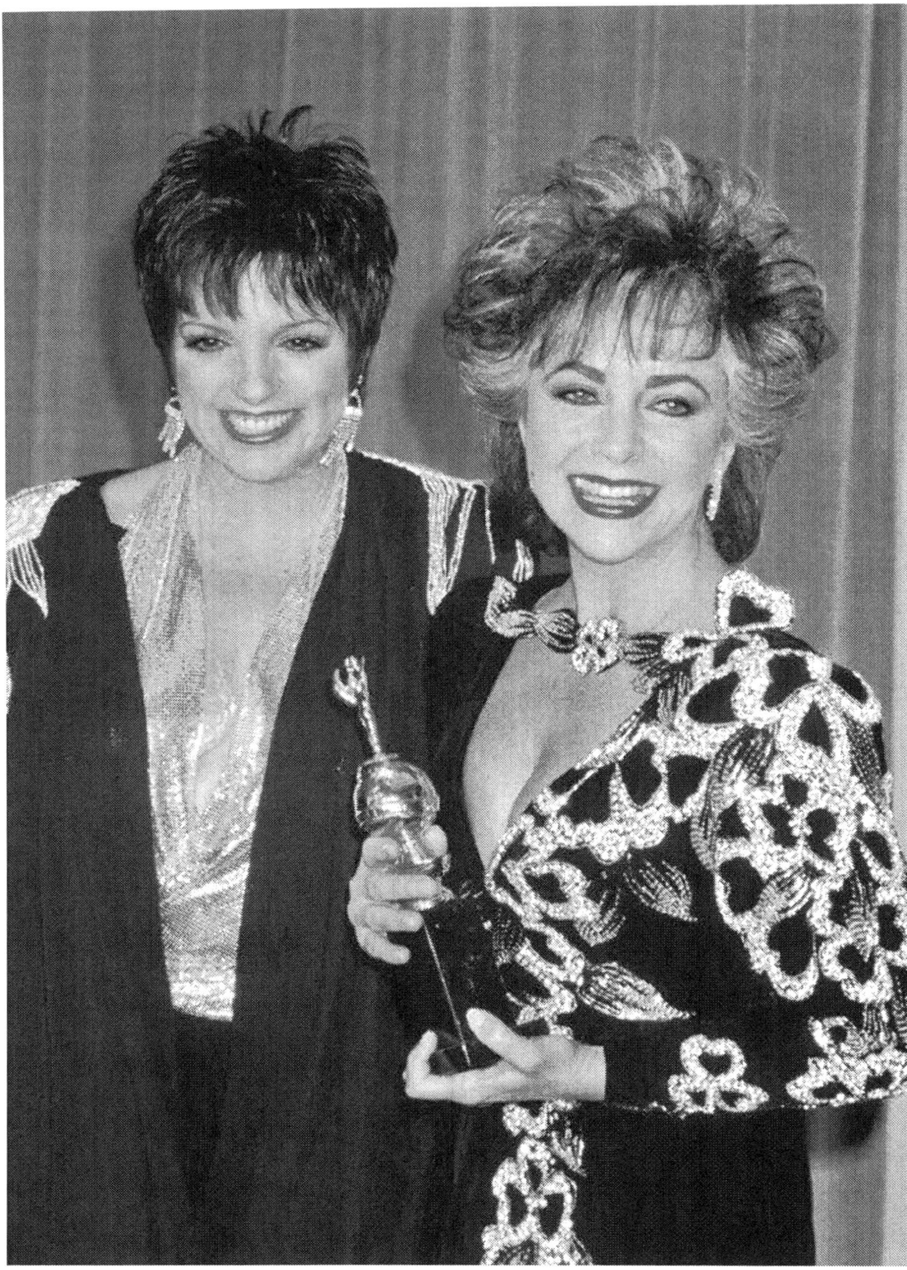

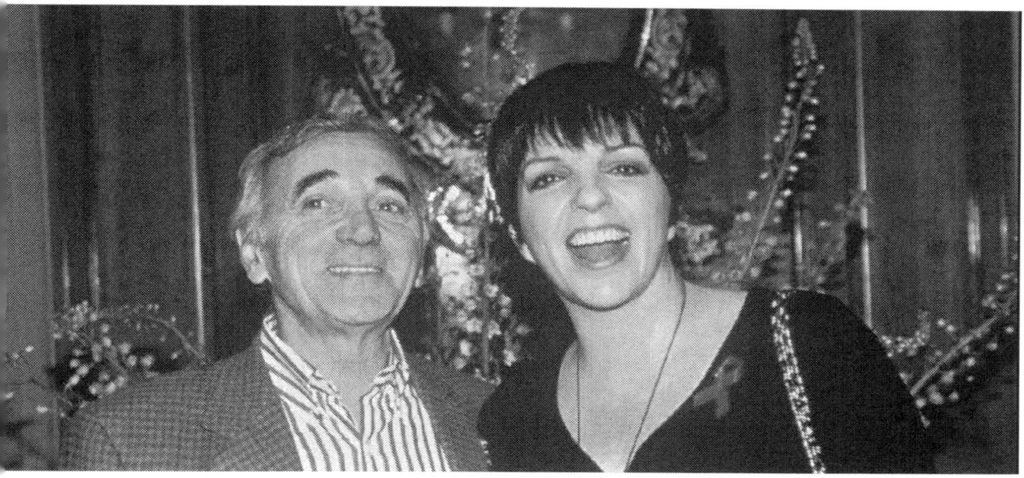

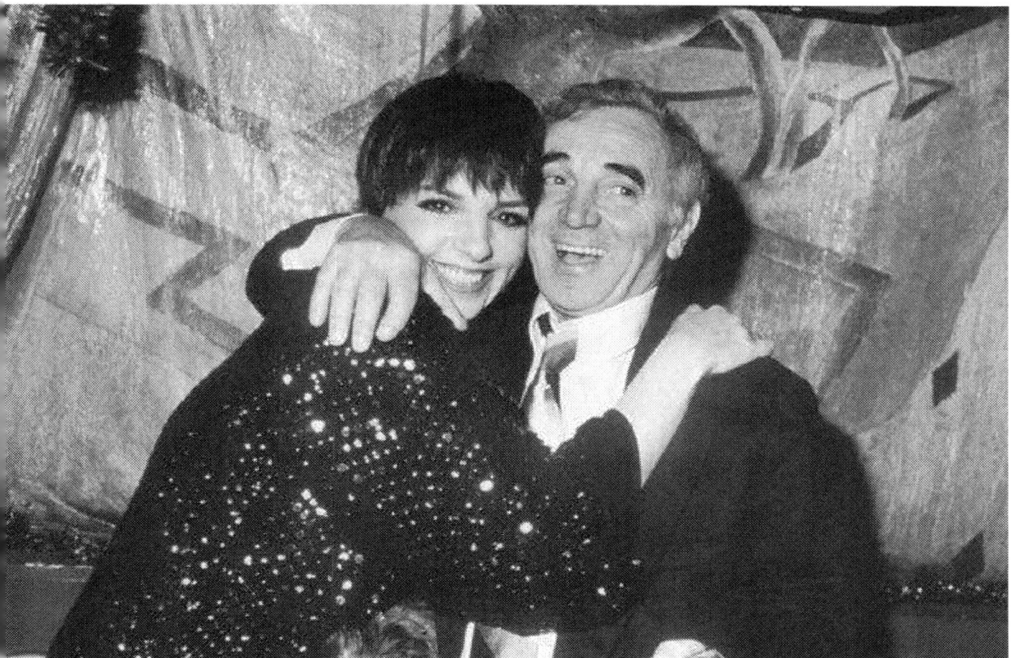

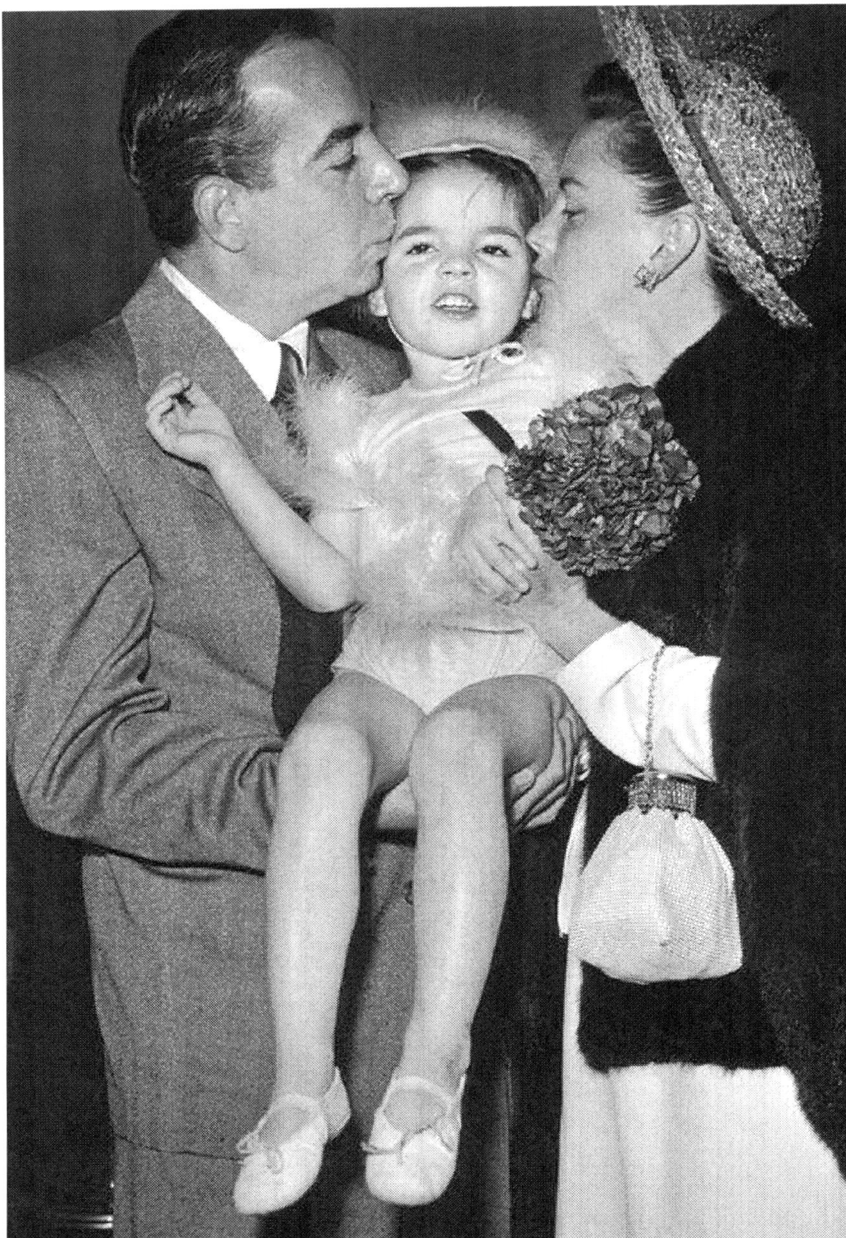

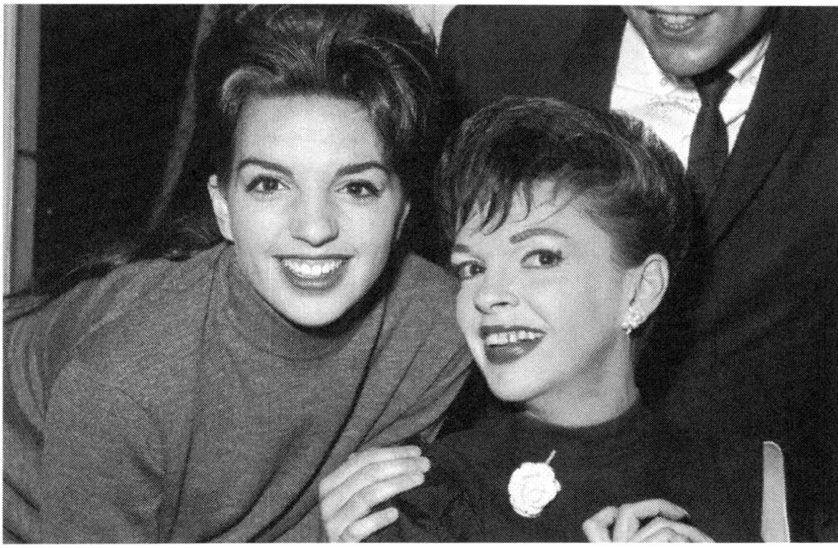

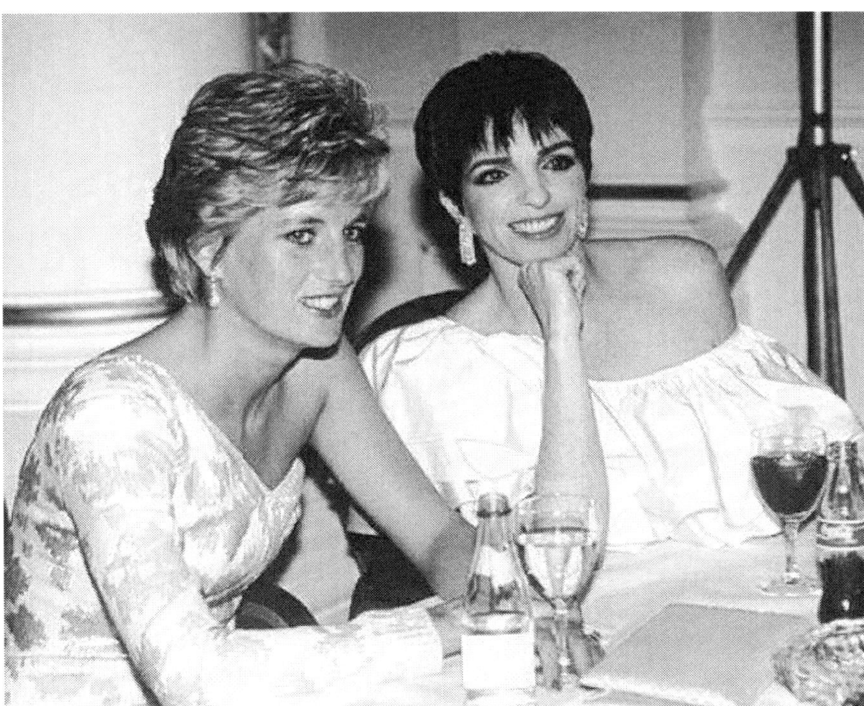

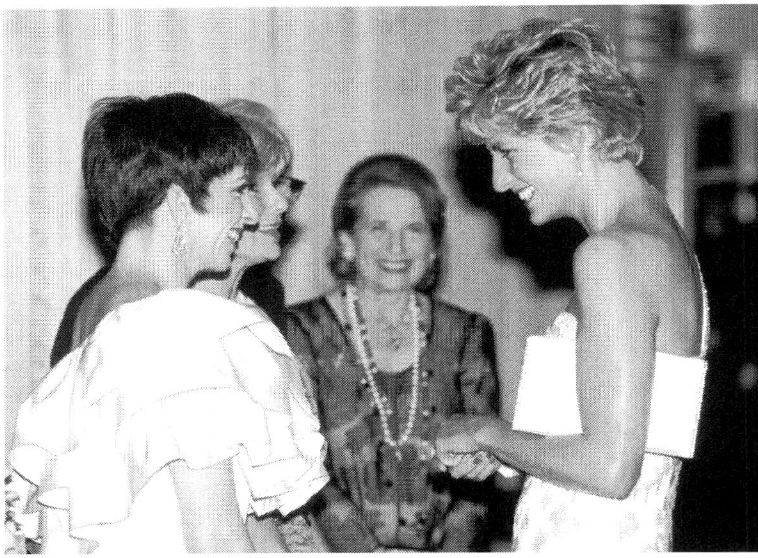

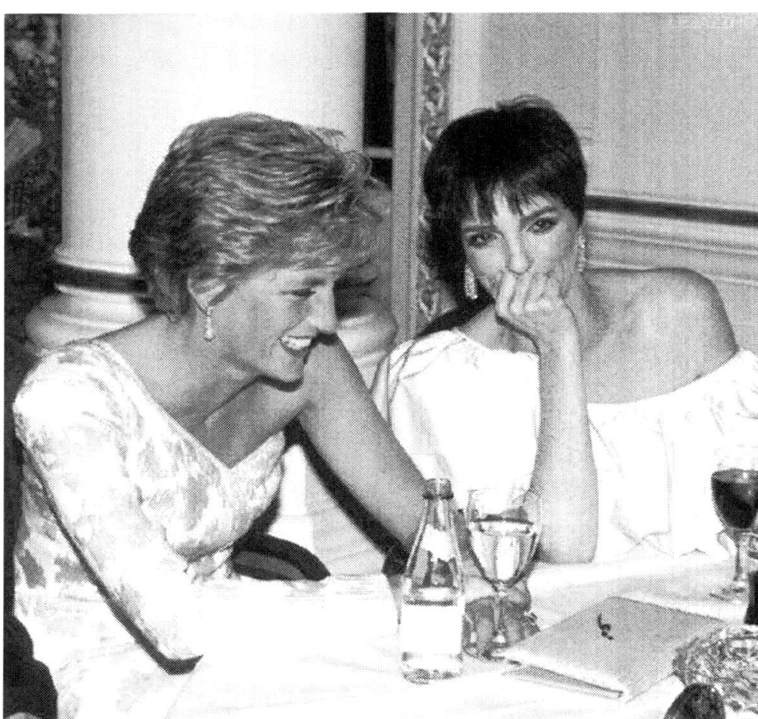

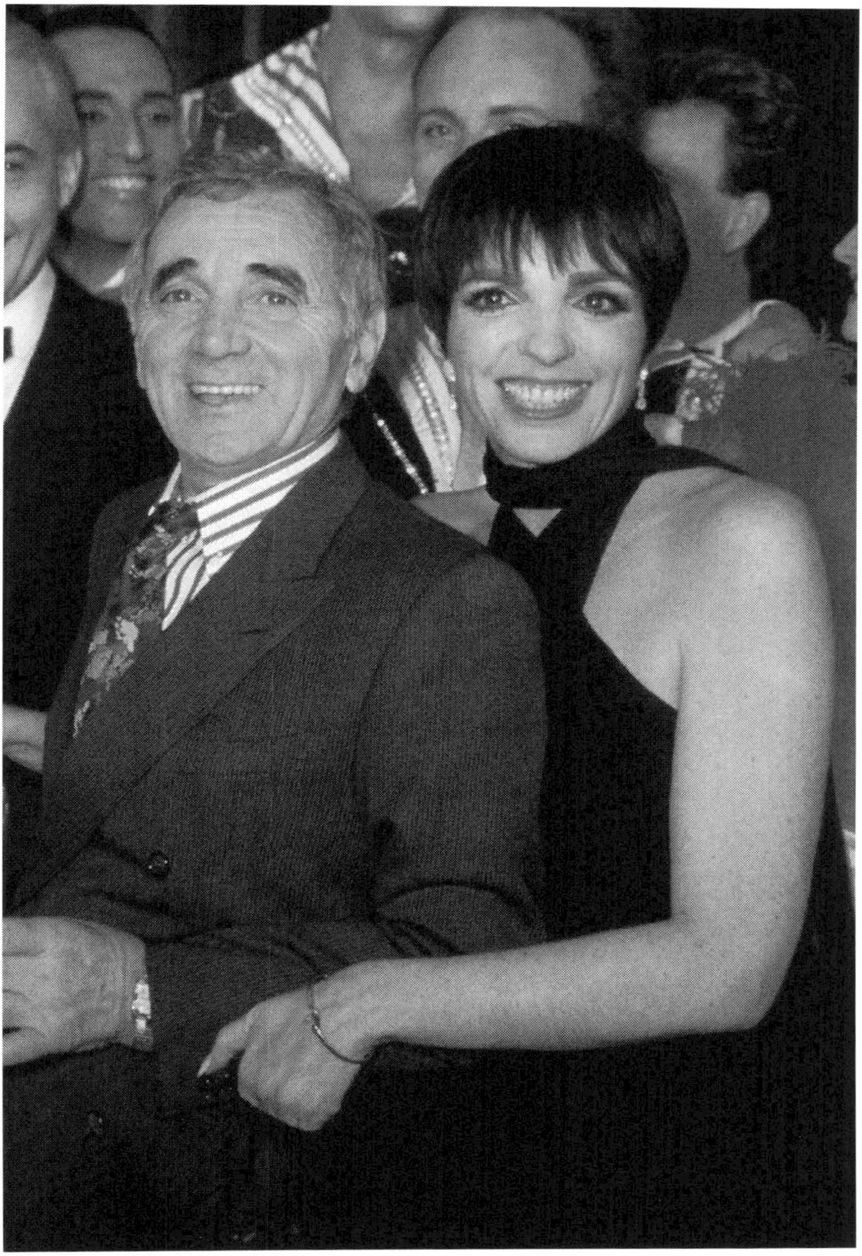

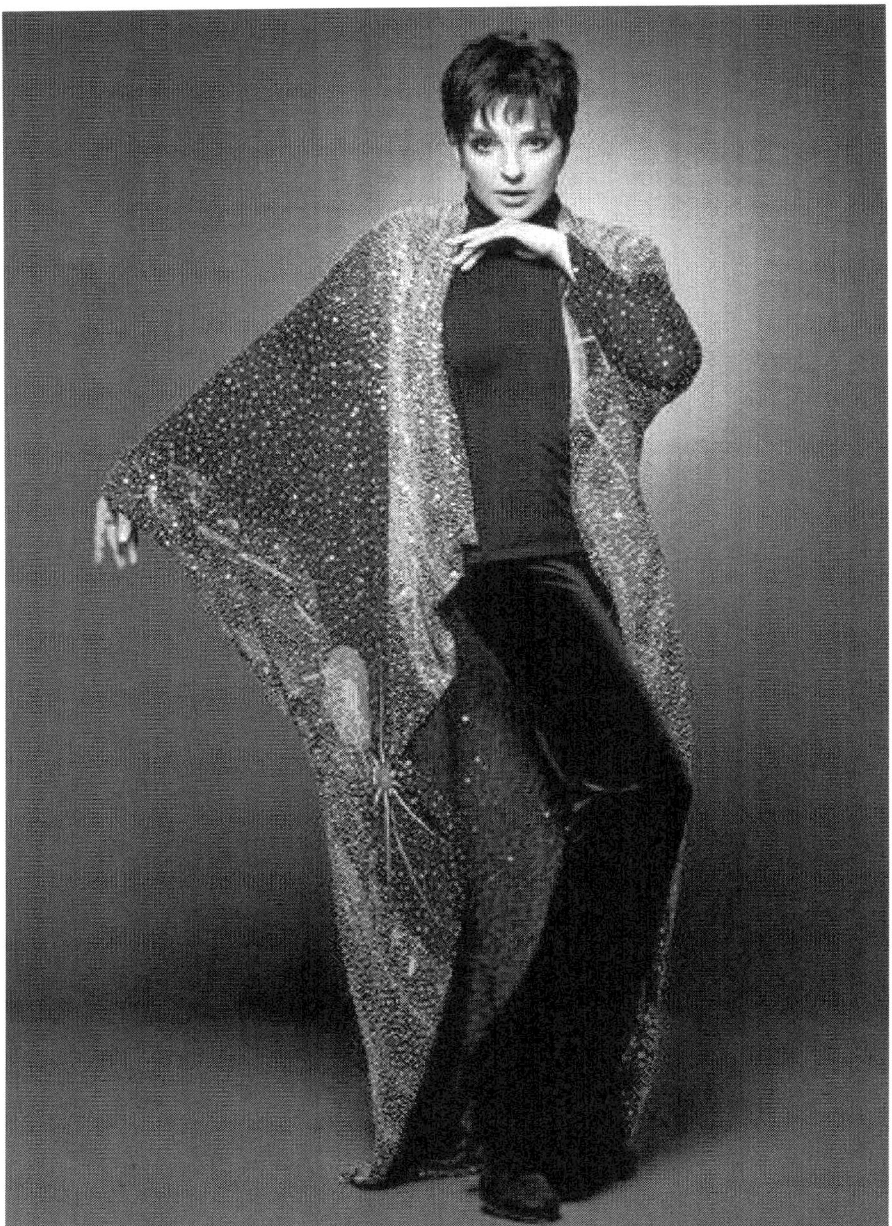

Printed in Great Britain
by Amazon